D1526348

Great Lent & Me

SAINT SHENOUDA PRESS

Great Lent & Me

Fr Bishoy Kamel

Translated By
Yvonne Tadros

ST SHENOUDA PRESS
SYDNEY, AUSTRALIA
2018

Great Lent & Me

ST SHENOUDA PRESS
8419 Putty Rd,
Putty, NSW, 2330
Sydney, Australia

www.stshenoudapress.com

ISBN 13: 978-0-9945710-9-0

Translated by:
Yvonne Tadros

Contents

Translator's Note:

These sermons were written in colloquial Egyptian Arabic. I tried my best to translate them for the English reader according to English sentence structure, with adherence to meaning in the Arabic version and at the same time reflecting the spirituality therein, as this booklet is part of a series of sermons by the Rev. Hegumenos Bishoy Kamel. Proper nouns are transliterated. There may also be spelling variations.

Biblical Quote References are from NIV or NKJV depending on which is closest to the Arabic Version.

The Great Lent Journey

God's purpose in our lives

Our fasting and worship ought to be within the frame of the Divine Purpose in our lives. When humanity broke the precept , the nature of man was corrupted through sin. For the sake of salvation and through His utmost love and sacrifice; God sent His only Son, Jesus Christ. His Son descended to our world, took our nature and became one of us. He walked with us through the path of salvation; was baptized in the Jordan River; fasted; was tested; laboured; He carried the cross; He died, resurrected and resurrected us with Him.

The cost of our salvation is beyond human imagination. God saved us from sin, liberated us from Satan's servitude, and not only that, He made us His children. He wants us to be successful and sanctified through His Holy Spirit and through His holy body and blood, and similar to all fathers, He wants us to be perfect "Be perfect, therefore, as your heavenly Father is perfect." (Matt 5:48)

God does not require of us perfect moral behaviour but rather He calles us to be His children. He is always compassionate towards us and constantly nurturing us with His body and blood. Thus, it would be a great loss on our behalf if we do not allow God to work His purpose in us.

In Summary, if Christianity required that a person to only be ethical, it would have been merely a philosophy or ideology. Christianity is Christ living within His children.

Christ does not hold us accountable for our sins, but for not repenting. Saint Nilous of Sinai states "God's purpose in our lives is that we be betrothed to Him as a pure chaste bride". Who does not wish to be the most beautiful bride?"

"you were thrown out into the open field, for on the day you were born you were despised...Then I passed by and saw you kicking about in your blood, and as you lay there in your blood.....I bathed you with water and washed the blood from you and put ointments on you. I clothed you with an embroidered dress and put sandals of fine leather on you. I dressed you in fine linen and covered you with costly garments. I adorned you with jewelry: I put bracelets on your arms and a necklace around your neck, and I put a ring on your nose, earrings on your ears and a beautiful crown on your head. So you were adorned with gold and silver; your clothes were of fine linen and costly fabric and embroidered cloth. Your food was honey, olive oil and the finest flour. You became very beautiful and rose to be a queen. And your fame spread among the nations on account of your beauty, because the splendor I had given you made your beauty perfect, declares the Sovereign Lord." -Ezekiel 16

What does God want from me?

God wants me to be His child, to walk in His path, to bear His countenance, His fragrance, His image, and within me have His strengths and meekness. He wants me to be a pure and chaste bride; pure in thoughts and heart, with thoughts focused only on Christ who is the centre of life, of the whole world - the centre of the blemish-free heart which is consecrated to the Lord.

He wants us to be participants in His divine nature "Through these he has given us his very great and precious promises, so that through them you may participate in the divine nature."(2Peter 1:4) This is God's purpose and through His Grace, I seek "Not that I have already obtained all this, or have already arrived at my goal, but I press on to take hold of that for which Christ Jesus took hold of me." (Phil.3:12). This is the purpose of Lent.

We are required to be pure, which is not part of our nature, nor is it within our ability, rather it is only of God's nature, who purified us through His Holy Spirit. We are required to grow spiritually. We are required to grow in love to the point that we offer the left cheek and the extra mile, which is not within our ability, but is within Jesus' ability who gives us His own self to carry out His own work.

The belief at the start of Lent

The precept is hard and some would describe it as hypothetical. Actually it is very difficult for humans, but very easy for Christ who dwells within us. This is the secret of our Christianity. We do not carry out the precept through our own effort, but through Christ who dwells within us, "Remain in me, as I also remain in you."

(John 15:4) Thus, we are able to carry out the hardest instruction that "I can do all things [which He has called me to do] through Him who strengthens and empowers me" (Philipians 4:13), because what is impossible with man is possible with God. This is our faith that Christ tells us about, also when He tells us "Therefore I tell you, whatever you ask for in prayer, believe that you have received it, and it will be yours." (Mark 11:24)

The start of Lent is the discovery of this essential doctrinal fact. When Saint Abu Maqar witnessed a scene of sin he did not judge the sinner but he fell on his face and prayed. He then heard a voice saying: "Abu Maqar you are becoming like God. You witness people's faults and you cover up for them". Another example from the life of this saint, during a famine someone gave his last loaf of bread to someone who asked him, and because of this act, God sent rain to alleviate the famine [which was caused by a drought].

Let us fast and follow Christ's example, to fulfill His calling for us to be saints and light to the world. We should never be anything less than what He has called us to be.

What is Lent?

Following His Baptism, the Lord fasted. Fasting,

combined with prayer and faith, form the means through which one may fulfill God's purpose. Who among us does not wish to fulfill God's purpose? Christ himself fasted. He fasted on our behalf, paying in advance a deposit for our own fasting so that when we fast, He is our partner in the journey of fasting. He set the plan, now He is our partner in it.

Fasting is not an excercise in suffering for the body, rather a liberation of the spirit in order to enjoy the companionship of Jesus during the walk to Gethsemane, then the Golgotha ending with dawn of Resurrection and culminating with the glory of the divine ascension, when the ultimate purpose is fulfilled.

Preparation Week

Preparation Sunday

The first Sunday of the Lenten period is commonly known as 'Sunday of the Preparation for Abstinence' or 'Preparation Sunday' and today's readings were under the theme of 'Preparation for Abstinence'. This is the week that we fast before the forty days of the Great Lent.

Common Themes through Preparation Week

Throughout Preparation Week if one is to attend the services the common themes of the readings would be:

Tolerance, Forgiveness and Love

These themes alternate throughout this week i.e. "Our Father... Forgive us our trespasses as we forgive those who trespass against us."

Preparation week

This week which precedes the Great Lent (supposedly 40 days), and one may contemplate that the general Christian practice is to fast forty days. So why does the Coptic Church have an additional week prior to the Great Lent? Does one prepare for fasting with more fasting?

The issue here is not one of fasting. When we fast, our fasting needs to be favourably received. If it is not, then it is worthless. Without the practice of self-control and discipline alongside the virtues of Tolerance, Forgiveness and Love, fasting would be pointless.

Fasting will not have any impact if you do not discipline yourself spiritually in advance. If you do not learn forgiveness and tolerance, your fasting is fruitless.

Right from the start, the Church in her wisdom made it clear that the readings are not limited only to the Vesper Gospel, but include the Gospel of Matine.

The theme of the Gospel Reading of the day after Preparation Sunday will be about the well known verses of "Our Father.... Forgive us our trespasses as we forgive those who trespass against us." Clearly my brothers and sisters 'Preparation for Fasting' means Forgiveness.

When Christ says "Be Careful", it is always a caution. It means to 'Watch Out'. If someone trespasses against you, and repents - forgive them. To 'be careful' equals 'watch out' is a severe caution that needs to be reiterated. If someone trespasses against you seven times and seeks your forgiveness seven times, then forgive them.

I was sitting with someone and I don't know how it happened that a thought occurred to me. I thought aloud "What is greatest about Christianity? What is the greatest act anyone can do?" The Lord led both of us to the answer: it is to forgive. We placed before our eyes the image of Jesus Christ who forgave the whole human race, because the whole human race transgressed against Him. Therefore, when our Lord forgave, forgiveness was not free. For a person to forgive, one must overlook status, pride and dignity. And the greater the transgression, the greater is the sacrifice – exponentially greater. Just imagine that it was infinitely greater that the price was Jesus' death, and that is the ultimate in terms of forgiveness.

Do you think forgiveness is free? No. It has a price. Because for someone who is insulted, and whose pride is hurt, how can they forgive? In the epistle to the Colossians 2:14, saint Paul mentioned that on the cross Jesus paid our debt in full "... having wiped out the handwriting of requirements that was against us, which was contrary to us. And He has taken it out of the way, having nailed it to the cross."

Forgiveness, my brothers and sisters, cost Christ His blood. Constantly bear this in mind, always remember FORGIVENESS = CHRIST'S BLOOD. This is the concept that we ought to embrace in our lives as God's children.

Forgiveness is not merely a word to be used casually such as "X forgave Y" and then that is the end of the story. No, not so. As Christians, our understanding of forgiveness came only through Christ's blood, and in that regard, none of us knows how to forgive. Only Christ knows the depth of the word; so much so, that He simplified the concept in the parable of the two men: one who owed 50 denarii and another who owed 500 denarii. (Matt 18:21-35)

When the one who owed the 500 was forgiven his debt, this same man had someone owing him 50. So, he went, grabbed him and demanded repayment of the 50. When he could not repay, and despite his pleading the lender, and the very same man who was forgiven, sent him to prison.

When the lender of the 500 who waived the debt heard of the story, he called him:

"You wicked servant! I forgave you all that debt because you begged me. Should you not also have had compassion on your fellow servant, just as I had pity on you?' And his master was angry, and delivered him to the torturers until he should pay all that was due to him."

As a matter of fact, in Christianity 'forgiveness' has a totally different definition. It is not confined to conflicts among parties whereby all ends up with reconciliation. Forgiveness in Christianity is the feeling of peace because the loan of 500 is from Christ. Let us assume that I am the borrower, and I am owed 50, or 20, or 10 or even 5.... And then? Do you see my point? I need to be careful before claiming, lest the Lender insists on also claiming his 500 from me.

That is why forgiveness in Christianity is conditional: "forgive us our trespasses as we..." If you complete the verse you will understand the clause which is the basis of the condition.

There was an incident involving Bishop Anba Abraam, Bishop of Fayoum, when he had to listen to details of a conflict between two parties, who came to him seeking counsel. He listened to them and tried to placate them through his preaching. However, it was all in vain.

He told them: "Alright then, let us all stand up for prayer". He began with the Lord's Prayer: "Our Father, who is in Heaven... forgive us our trespasses." He paused, then continued "…. and forgive us NOT our trespasses, as we DO NOT forgive those who trespassed against us".

The conflicting parties stopped him saying: "how can you say that... no, no, don't say that".

The Bishop said "What do you mean 'don't say that' are we being hypocritical? He knows that we did not forgive". After hearing this, they were embarrassed and reconciled.

The first point, which I wish to be embossed in the depth, of our souls is; it was not we who initiated forgiveness but we were forgiven beyond imagination. That is why one is unable to raise one's eyes towards our Lord nor stand before Him in prayer, unless we forgive; because The Lord was the one who began the forgiving - and when he forgave, He did so abundantly.

The Vesper Gospel has a wonderful connection with the Dawn Gospel, which addresses:

• Prayer;

• Forgiveness; and

• Faith

One may ask: What is the correlation?

Actually the correlation of prayer and forgiveness is clear, because in prayer one communicates with Christ, and how do I communicate? Clearly, I must have forgiven. If I have not, myself, forgiven how can I ask Him to forgive me? How can I seek if my attitude with my friends were to be "I won't forgive, I won't talk to you, I won't forgo not even a cent".

It is apparent that in Christianity, there is a very serious, deep and fundamental correlation between prayer and forgiveness. Prayer is not favourably received without forgiveness. Meaning that the word "forgiveness" is crossed out. The emphasis is that when one stands for prayer, the individual and God are on good terms: that one is truly in communion with Him, with a genuine connection.

"And when you stand praying, if you hold anything

against anyone, forgive them, so that your Father in heaven may forgive you your sins." (Mark 11:25) This verse is a conditional promise, or even a warning.

Conclusion on Forgiveness and Prayer

The first point is now adequately covered and it goes without saying Christianity is Forgiveness, which by now is embossed within our hearts. This can be summarised by the following: we are forgiven beyond measure and now we realize this fact, we do not need persuasion. Others may say to us "How can you do that? You have every right... You suffered... etc." You will find that within yourself you have the inner peace of knowing you are only trying to reciprocate the forgiveness given to you. Outsiders won't understand this concept, only those who are in communion with God.

Secondly, prayer is the core of Christianity "Then He spoke a parable to them, that men always ought to pray and not give up." (Luke 18:1). Jesus spoke several parables about prayer. However, we are weak when it comes to fervent prayer - the least we can do is stand before God even in this weak state but with a forgiving heart, we will be well received by God.

Belief and forgiveness

Surprisingly, tonight's Vesper and the Dawn Gospel are a combination of "Belief" and "Forgiveness". What is the correlation?

Jesus said that the Christian belief is not mere talk, because this type of belief, which is prevalent in the world at present, is demonic belief. "You believe that God is one; you do well. Even the demons believe—and shudder!" (James 2:19). In a way, demons' belief is better than ours because "they shudder!" If you happen to talk to someone about 'Belief' one will tell you "Of course, I believe in our Lord. I believe in the existence of God, in my faith, in my doctrine... and on.... and on" ... No.

For sometime, some Christians have been adopting a very serious hypothesis regarding Christianity i.e. "Christianity is not a demonic faith. Christianity is pragmatic and this is even confirmed by Apostle James who. They further quote (James 2:18) "But someone will say, 'You have faith; I have deeds'. Show me your faith without deeds, and I will show you my faith by my deeds" continuing in their argument, they say "I don't have to tell you I am a believer - my deeds will tell you."

Why is forgiveness attached to Christian belief? Because the Christian belief is founded on this basis: Christ died on the cross and forgave us our sins. This is our sole belief, and no other. Our belief is one of forgiveness, and if I do not believe, then my belief is doubtful and not as solid as described in the verse: "Truly I tell you, if anyone says to this mountain, 'Go, throw yourself into the sea,' and does not doubt in their heart but believes that what they say will happen, it will be done for them." (Mark 11:23)

Definition of belief (Faith)

What is the meaning of "We believe"?

- We believe in the death of Christ on the cross and why?
- We believe: for the forgiveness of our sins

We believe in the forgiveness of sins; consequently, if we believe in forgiveness, the Christian Belief is to be placed in its "pragmatic frame" which is forgiveness.

Belief in the shed blood: irrespective of the magnitude of the sin, it can be forgiven. The belief that Christ's blood purifies all sins; our Lord forgives all sins as described in the return of the Prodigal Son whereupon his father embraced him. The whole belief is based on forgiveness.

The practical way of experiencing the impact of Christ's blood upon a Christian believer's life is the extent of one's forgiveness towards others. If a person feels that they are forgiven, it means that they constantly sense Christ's forgiveness and this is Belief/Faith.

Therefore, if Vesper Theme on the Sunday during preparation week is about 'Belief', then we mean "Belief" in Christ's blood which purifies us from sin.

Now we know the main point as to why we call our prelude to the Great Lent "Preparation Week". Clearly, it is not the actual start of the Great Lent.

Fatherhood

One of the vitally important points and which we will clarify even further tomorrow is:

"For if you forgive others their trespasses, your heavenly Father will also forgive you, but if you do not forgive others their trespasses, neither will your Father forgive your trespasses."

The point of focus in the mentioned verse is "your heavenly Father" because it reflects a new meaning of God being a "Father/your Father".

Preparation for fasting is understanding the depth of the 'Filial Concept' which means that a person is not interacting with an unknown god, but with the Heavenly Father who holds genuine paternal feelings.

The expression 'Fatherhood' and the interaction on the level of Fatherhood/Filially are totally new, never known before, as it was a concept not resent in the Judaic faith. Up to this day people find it hard to believe that God is a Father.

We are not dealing with a ruthless and unjust god, nor are we being treated as employees who at the end of the day have to account for their work, to be assessed and then are sent to Paradise with phrases or sentences similar to "well done, now go, eat and drink and have fun as a reward for your hard day's work, this is your pay for the day". No, not so. We are treated on the level of a filial relationship. You will see this reflected throughout the whole of the Great Lent period. For example: on the third Sunday, I will be speaking about the Prodigal Son and the father who rushes to embrace him with open arms, kissing him the whole time. The whole parable is about fatherhood, the tender love and warmth flowing from his father's bosom and his kisses. It covers the core of a fatherly love, which we reflect on when we fast, pray and when we are charitable, all this as part of interaction with "our Father who is in Heaven".

Do not do things for the sake of pleasing people but seek pleasing "your Father who is in Heaven". When a Christian enjoys the sweet taste of forgiveness, the feeling of being in our Lord's warm bosom and the feeling of interaction with a father, these fulfilling feelings are in contrast with the insatiable feeling of a person who lives aimlessly in life who does not know where to go or what to do to have satisfaction. As a matter of fact there is nothing in this life to satisfy the human desires whether it is money, enjoyment, food, drink, the list goes on. All these worldly pleasures are nowhere near the true joy of being in communion with God.

Actually, one has to be very careful during Preparation Week. For example, if you are preparing for a long-distance journey, you take time to prepare for it. You start by getting a suitcase, organizing your documents and continue with your planning for preparation, thinking: "I am traveling on a long journey. I have to be well prepared for the journey". Without preparing, it would be recklessness, because you may leave and midway, you discover you had forgotten the necessities to sustain you on your travels. Even Christ, in one of His parables gave the example of the foolish builder who could not complete the tower because he had not made his calculations ahead, thus becoming ridiculed for being unable to have the foresight to complete his task (Luke 14:28-30).

The significance of "Preparation Week"

It is the week of preparing sustenance for the journey. The journey of the Great Lent is a long one. If you do not combine it with faith, you will weaken when you hunger and when you deprive yourself in penance. However, if you believe that "This kind can come out by nothing but prayer and fasting" (Mark 9:29); and prayer and fasting shield against temptation, thus elevating our spirits to our Father's bosom, the whole church will enjoy the peace of crushing Satan under our feet, which is evidenced in the Temptation on the Mount (Matt 4:8).

Sequence of the Weeks of the Great Lent:

i. Temptation on the Mount

ii. The Prodigal Son

iii. Meeting the Samaritan Woman at the Well

iv. The healing of the (38 years) quadriplegic

v. Restoration of Vision to the Blind Man

vi. Palm Sunday

If you believe in the concepts of each of the above sequence, what each week represents from the Temptation right to "Hosannah King of Israel" followed by "Tell it out among the nations, that the Lord reigns from the wood" which is the Cross (the end of the journey) you will realize we do not have anyone reigning over our hearts, no one else other than Jesus. Our joy, my dear friends, culminates at the end of this journey.

I hope that I clarified in your minds the significance of the Preparation Week. It is a sustenance week, which prepares you for the journey, lest you weaken on the way. If you travel without forgiveness, without the feeling that God is your Father and you are enjoying His paternity, you will falter mid way.

May our Good Lord bless this week, and prepare us to be worthy of the grace and blessing of this Holy Great Lent.

Treasures in Heaven

The Second Sunday of the Great Lent.

The Lord Jesus draws our attention to a very important instruction to Christians: and that is the life of submission to God. He begins his teaching, "Therefore do not worry about tomorrow, for tomorrow will worry about itself. Each day has enough trouble of its own." (Matt 6:34)

Our Lord Jesus knows that by nature, the human being is a worrier, and this creates instability in one's spiritual and psychological life and the weakening of faith, which also leads to physical problems.

Our Lord Jesus Christ at the first week of the Lent

teaches us not to worry. He tells us not to worry about tomorrow. In chapter six of the Gospel reading of St. Matthew, which is read during Sunday mass, we learn the extent of God's love and care for us.

You will listen to examples of the lilies in the fields "Yet I tell you that not even Solomon in all his splendour was dressed like one of these."(Matt 6:26) Also, examples of God's care and vigilance, which extends to the birds in the sky "Look at the birds of the air; they do not sow or reap or store away in barns, and yet your heavenly Father feeds them. Are you not much more valuable" (Matt 6:26) and other similar examples to show us not to worry.

Ask anyone: what is the main concern of people these days? They well tell you the greatest illness is anxiety or fear. The fear of the unknown or the fear of the future. Jesus knows that because the human life rotates around the demands of the body, anxiety also rotates around the same concern, even though we may imagine that our concerns are about moral issues in the world, but deep down they are about our bodily needs.

For this reason, Lent is becomes beneficial to the body as it is not a matter of eating and drinking. We should not think that the whole blessing of Lent is abstinence from food and a swap from one diet to another. There is no such concept. Jesus knows that the needs of the body are of great concern to us, and that is why he asks us not to be overly concerned with our bodily needs. He created that body, He knows its needs and He provides those needs.

Do not be anxious about tomorrow:

As mentioned earlier in this chapter: anxiety is a spiritual and emotional disorder, because it is compounded by fear that also affects us physically. You may notice that one of the ailments of the twentieth century are neurological disorders that become physically manifested. For example: "butterflies" in the stomach when one is nervous. When you ask "What causes all this?" The answer is: anxiety.

Therefore anxiety becomes a part of daily life.

Christ reminds us: "Do not be anxious about tomorrow". An impulsive retort to this instruction may be "Do you mean I should not care? Should I be indifferent?" Christ takes us step by step in resolving our anxiety: "And which of you by being anxious can add one cubit unto the measure of his life? Which of you can change the colour of one hair from gray to black?" No one can add to their life by worrying. Our Lord emphasises: ""Indeed, the very hairs of your head are all numbered. Do not fear; you are more valuable than many sparrows." (Luke 12:7)

Conditons of Christ's fellowship

If we go back to the journey of the Disciples at the start of their mission, what were the conditions for that mission? The Disciples, who were committing themselves to evangelism throughout the world, what were their prerequisites: an education? Prestige?

Our Lord Jesus told them "Take nothing for your journey, no staff, nor bag, nor bread, nor money; and do not have two tunics" (Luke 9:3) In another Gospel he told them to take a staff, but the intended meaning was the "Pastoral Staff" similar to our Patriarch's or a Bishop's Pastoral Staff. It is merely a symbol of Pastorship.

Then, at one stage, they told Him it was hard. Then Jesus asked them, "When I sent you without purse, bag or sandals, did you lack anything?" They answered "nothing".

The Disciples possibly thought how they were to financially support their mission, their previous lives. They gave up everything to follow Christ. He told them they would receive guidance as to how to earn their living.

During Pentecost there no one was in need amongst the Disciples. For from time to time those who owned land or houses sold them, brought the money from the sales and put it at the Apostles' feet, and it was distributed to whomever had need.

The Church's view regarding finance

I recall in one of the Ecumenical Churches Council Conferences the theme was about finances. Each member represented their church view about finance and how they coped.

A Priest from Sweden said: "Our Church has its own Bank called 'Church Bank'. This Bank caters for the church needs." When the Coptic Church was asked "From where does the Parish Priest get money to feed himself?" We told them "A donation plate is passed around the congregation and this caters for the food of the priest and the deacons."

An important point was raised: "What if numbers of the congregation dwindle, from where will you get the money? The income will diminish." It was a logical point, but contrary to the teachings of Christ: "When I sent you without purse, bag or sandals, did you lack anything?" How can we now, being employed by The Lord, worry about how are we going to survive. Those helpless

Apostles who were poor fishermen, had money laid at their feet. They practically walked on it.

Later on, when problems of managing the finances grew within the Church, Peter stood up and told them ""Select from among you seven deacons to minister for the community. It is not right that we neglect the word of God and serve tables" (Acts 6:3). This was the early church.

The calibre of evangelism

"Any house you visit, eat what you are offered" (Luke 10:8). A sceptic disciple may argue that food may not be offered during their visitations. Jesus replies: "Go... I am the One who touches people's hearts. I send food even to birds. Go with a firm belief, and contribute towards the strengthening of the Church. Do not carry any staff on the way".

The sceptic may further argue, "What if we are attacked by a dog or bear or any other beast, what shall we do in self-defence?" Christ would say "in such a case, this will be the introduction to your evangelism. One of you may go and on the way and a lion attacks, similar to St. Mark's experience, who drew the sign of the cross towards the face of the lion and it fell down dead. St.Mark ran to the village and entered panting. When they asked him about his problem and the purpose of his visit, he explained that is was to evangelise. In answering their curiosity about the nature of this evangelism, he did not have a long introduction: the proof was there - he told them about what had happened to him on his way to them. He told them the whole story, adding that he did not even have to carry a staff. This added to their surprise: how can one walk through the desert without carrying a staff? He explained to them "My teacher taught me so. I should not carry any staff. As soon as I drew the sign of the cross, the lion died." That was the introduction to St. Mark's evangelism. He did not have to elaborate on preaching about the Lord being with us, or His protection, or that he is our Shepherd even if we do not carry our staff.

During the era of the Old Testament, the Lord fed His people, cared for them, gave them victory in wars and many other things. In the New Testament, He gives us Himself "And behold, I am with you always, to the end of the age."

Our Preacher Apostle St. Paul said not to be concerned with anything at all, except for one thing: Prayer. We are commanded to "pray without ceasing" (1 Thessalonians 5:16). God knows our needs. We need to feel our Lord's presence with us when we pray, whereby we place everything in His hands and so, adding to our belief in

His constant care: "Come to me, all you who are weary and burdened, and I will give you rest". (Matt 11:28)

When the Disciples did not carry a staff, the Lord fought on their behalf against wild beasts: their faith became much, much deeper. When they did not carry money, and money was placed at their feet: their faith became much, much deeper.

For this reason, my beloved, we are now in an age where everything is subject to "Insurance". Life insurance, insurance for this, insurance for that and insurance for everything. Even the Priest has to be insured. All this is good, and we say "Look how the church is well organised, everything is now systematic". However, consequent to all this, faith is on the decline, because materialistic insurance gives some sense of reassurance.

When Jesus taught His disciples, He did not do so as a type of detachment, or to place them in a difficult position. Never. He did so meaning "I am the one who will care for you. I will carry your burden. You do not have to worry about anything "But seek first his kingdom and his righteousness, and all these things will be given to you as well." (Matt 6:33)

If there is anything you need to worry about, it is the salvation of your soul. Our Lord quoted parables in the simplest way,"What will you gain if you gain the whole world and lose your soul?" (Matt 16:26) Ask yourself, which is better?

But who will pay heed?

A moment of reflection: truly, what will a person gain if one gains the whole world and loses one's soul? When he asked us not to worry about tomorrow, he went further and added "But seek first God's Kingdom and His righteousness"

According to Christianity, Jesus' gift to us is unmatched. One may ask: In what way is it unmatched? My dear friend, He gave us Himself - His own body and blood and blessed us with his Spirit dwelling within us. What more could we ask for?

Forgive us O Lord, we have sinned against you, and against ourselves when we worried mainly about our wellbeing, about our future, about our children, about their future. Lord, if only we entrusted YOU with all our burdens. If we only believed in your promise that all what we asked would be given and even more.

When preaching to the Corinthians St. Paul asked them as to what were they complaining about, as if they had received nothing while they received everything: as they had received Christ. Was there anything more? God did not withhold His own self, what more could anyone ask for?

That is why my beloved, these days it is so hard to tell you not to worry. Your immediate response will be "Father, I can't help it. With the state of affairs and life these days, I just can't help it". I still repeat, don't worry, you have Christ on your side and it is the same God, yesterday, today and forevermore: "I have set the Lord always before me; because He is at my right hand, I shall not be shaken." (Psalms 16:8)

I think   adequately covered this point regarding the fulfilment of your needs as explained earlier. In summary, do not worry about the bag, the money, the food nor the staff. Your main and only concern is to seek God's Kingdom and His righteousness.

Focus on being attached to God. This is what will give you reassurance throughout your life.

The greatest threat in your life is being detached from God. In the Christian understanding the corporal, or bodily, death is not the real death; it is being detached from God.

The path towards strong faith

i. THE MATERIALISTIC MEDIAN

I wish to focus on this particular point. I will call it "The Materialistic Median" i.e. the "Materialistic Needs Median" This is a path of faith-strengthening; or the medium through which God interacts with us, in order to elevate our faith in Him. Meaning, He subtracts a little and adds a little, and this is a Divine Equation; it does not mean that God is toying with us. The main factor in this equation is not to be detached from God.

ii. ORDEALS

Among the main sources of concern in this world are the trials we suffer. This is a lengthy subject, "trials breed anxiety". In the Old Testament, trials represented God forsaking the human race, leading to their being subject to ordeals. However, in the New Testament, St. James tells us: "Count it all joy, my brothers, when you meet trials of various kinds, for you know that the testing of your faith produces steadfastness. And let steadfastness have its full effect, that you may be perfect and complete, lacking in nothing." (James 1:2) Therefore, now we are in the age of Grace.

When God allows trials, He does so according to one's endurance; in other words He tailors according to size so not to lead an individual to despair and sin and there are several examples of this.

• If you ask the three young men about their experience during their ordeal inside the furnace, what would their answer be? It would be "We were in God's company. He was with us";

• Ask the Apostle Paul about his experience in the Philippian prison. He will tell you: "I saw the Lord with my own eyes". And then, what about outside the Prison? "I didn't see anything, the Prison gates became wide open, and the Prison Guard wanted to kill himself with his sword. I told him not to, that none of the prisoners had escaped and we were all still there. He took us to his home. We baptized his family, he gave us food, washed our wounds, and as you see we are here"

• Ask Paul how did the stoning ordeal affect him? He will tell you "This particular ordeal elevated me to the third heavens "I know a man in Christ who fourteen years ago was caught up to the third heaven. Whether it was in the body or out of the body I do not know - God knows. And I know that this man - whether in the body or apart from the body I do not know, but God knows - was caught up to paradise and heard inexpressible things, things that no one is permitted to tell." (2 Corinthians 12:2)

Christ said: "By your endurance you will gain your life" (Luke 21:19). He also said "But the one who endures to the end will be saved." (Matt 24:13) Then you ask "Until when?" St. Paul teaches us that ordeals produce endurance, and endurance is very important in the spiritual life. It is vital, it is the gateway which leads to Heaven and through which the Holy Spirit and the love of our Lord are poured into our hearts.

God's purpose VS our ordeals

Therefore, the important issue now in respect of worrying: It is trying to perceive what is our Lord's purpose behind a trial. What is He after? Possibly your answer would be: How would I know? Do I have a crystal ball? I tell you, you are able to perceive it. Apostle Paul could. He said: "And we know that God causes all things to work together for good to those who love God, to those who are called according to His purpose."

We are unable to perceive this statement, nor are we able to perceive God's mysteries, but believe me it is a fact, and because we trust in God, we come to realize this at a later stage.

"Most gladly, therefore, I will rather boast about my

weaknesses, so that the power of Christ may dwell in me. Therefore I am well content with weaknesses, with insults, with distresses, with persecutions, with difficulties, for Christ's sake; for when I am weak, then I am strong."

Apostle Paul continues to say that his experience with the LORD during his ordeals went much, much beyond his weakness. Thus, he rejoiced through ordeals and pains. This is Christianity and that is why we are called "Christians".

One day we were talking about our LORD'S "purpose". All of us reached the same conclusion: for the salvation of our souls. In a nutshell, this is His Purpose, and for you and me it is not being, for example, a Prime Minister or General Manager or any similar worldly high profile.

Rightous Joseph: The salvation of his soul and leading others to the salvation of their souls.

When Joseph went to see how his brothers were doing, they threw him in a well. When he was rescued from the well by strangers and sold to the Egyptians, he worked as a servant. Later on, he was falsely accused of a crime he did not commit and was thrown in prison.

However, we must not forget that God was preparing

him, first and foremost, to be the symbol of Christ who came to care for the wellbeing of His brethren in this world, but was wounded by his own beloved. Joseph was the reason behind the rescue from the famine that affected the whole Middle East nations. This was through the divine purpose and wisdom bestowed upon him.

I repeat, our Lord's purpose is the salvation of our souls. Hence, why worry? The real death is being detached from our Lord. Never sever your relationship with Christ. This is the greatest concern; even ordeals are blessing in disguise. Someone likens ordeals to baking a loaf of bread. The Baker kneads and keeps kneading the dough, leaves it on the tray and goes to sleep while it takes its leavening time. He awakes fully when it is time to prepare and heat the oven; and while the bread is inside the oven, the baker monitors the bread and when the it is ready, he takes it out whole and perfectly baked.

Our faith is tested by ordeals, similar to gold which is purified by fire.

Now we know that for our normal daily life we come across:

i. The Bag, the Sustenance and the Staff;

ii. Ordeals - giving rise to worrying/anxiousness;

iii. Third and final point: Anxiety

Anxiety may lead to sin. For example, you may come across someone who says to you "I am a lost cause. My youth is long gone and I did nothing good in my life towards God; I have a friend who is a monk, another one who is a bishop, and another one who did well and at the same time lead a life of prayer and here I am, a wasted life." This person dwells so much in the past and keeps harbouring negative thoughts, that he despairs and overlooks the fact that there is a future ahead.

I come across people who, during their confession, are so despondent that they think God may overlook any good deed they may have done. They forget the fact that Christ had come to blot our sins, that no one on earth can deprive us of His forgiveness. He does not wish that we surrender ourselves to despair, and from now on I do not want you to doubt "will God forgive me?" I want you to speak in the past tense "God forgave me".

Be sure your past was a debt repaid (in advance) on the cross. In other words, it is not still being paid by instalments. No. The debt was paid in advance, and in full - for your generation and for all future generations. The repayment is recorded individually for each one in their own account and is "settled in full".

I repeat, and will keep repeating, that our debts were paid in advance, and this means that we are FORGIVEN.

"But the gift is not like the trespass. For if the many died by the trespass of the one man, how much more did God's grace and the gift that came by the grace of the one man, Jesus Christ, overflow to the many!" (Romans 5:15-17) For this reason, it is not sin which is the Christian's main concern. I do not say so meaning that as a Christian, I am reckless. What I mean is that a Christian's heart is full of peace in the thought that my sins have been forgiven, blotted by Christ's blood. He told me not to worry about tomorrow, because He will handle it.

Often I come across people who tell me that they are constantly apprehensive about committing sins. I answer them "Pray each morning before leaving home. Ask God for guidance and say the following: "Lord Jesus, here I am surrendering myself to you. Help me through the day". He will keep you from the path of sin. He will lead you to a blessed future.

In his second epistle to the Ephesians, St. Paul tells us: "For we are God's handiwork, created in Christ Jesus to do good works, which God prepared in advance for us to do." (Ephesians 2:10)

You may question this and in rebuttal I say that you are bound to do good deeds because you are a member of Christ's body, and Christ's body does good only. It is automatic. Your movements follow this membership created in Christ Jesus to do good works. Your past is known Christ's Blood; your future is to do good works. However, what about the present? What are your plans for the present?

Focusing on Christ only

He is your portion "but one thing is necessary. Mary has chosen the good portion, which will not be taken away from her." This is the direction for the present I urge you to take, do not recall the past anymore, nor worry about the future because the past. Be reassured about the future. As to the present, intend to enjoy the fellowship of Christ. Try not to be distracted by worry. If Satan tries to remind me of the past say: "Disperse from me Satan, my past is gone without trace. It has been blotted by Christ's blood." Remember that your future is being a member of Christ's body to do good works. The present moment is joy and perfect peace because my life is constantly firm in Christ.

Therefore, my beloved, this anxiety which they describe as being the twentieth century greatest problem of all problems, believe me, the greatest of all problems is the spiritual state of mind for which they are unable to find a cure. Scientists are forever busy and active in attempts to find a cure for moodiness, depression, pain etc. They continue endlessly to invent sedatives to give some relief. Jesus gave us the prescription in one sentence "Do not worry about tomorrow."

Temptation on the Mount

The Third Sunday of the Great Lent.

At the beginning of the third week of the Holy Lent, the Gospel mentions the "Temptation of Christ on the Mountain". The church wishes that, as a congregation, we participate in communion with our Lord Jesus Christ during his fasting and also throughout his mission on earth.

We consider ourselves members of Christ's body. Whatever He did on earth was for our sake and also in partnership with us, because the Apostle states: "For we are members of His body, of His flesh, and of His bones." (Ephesians 5:30) The Church is the body of Christ who laid the foundation for His mission on Earth, which he applied and practised literally, and literality is not the intended meaning; that is to say literally practiced spirituality. Our Lord Jesus Christ is the Physician and Creator of our souls who knows the path leading to our salvation.

After fasting for forty days He was hungry. Although Jesus having a dual nature, that is human and divine, through His human nature was able to experience hunger as confirmed by the Gospel and after fasting for such a lengthy time was tempted by Satan "...and he was in the wilderness forty days, being tempted by Satan." (Mark 1:13).

Here we need to pause, as fasting during Lent involves hunger and temptation, but both go together hand in hand. For this reason we fast through complete abstinence, ie: "nil by mouth". It also involves "temptation", similar to Satan's words spoken to Christ during His fast, we face the same thoughts of temptation from Satan: You are getting weaker, you are hungry, your health is suffering, your circumstances do not allow fasting, your lifestyle does not allow and the list goes on.

An example from the Old Testament in Exodus 16:4,

"Then the Lord said to Moses, 'I will rain down bread from heaven for you. The people are to go out each day and gather enough for that day. In this way I will test them and see whether they will follow my instructions'" and in Psalms 78:23-25, "He rained down manna upon them to eat and gave them food from heaven. Man did eat the bread of angels; He sent them food in abundance."

God is capable of turning stones into bread and His miracles were manifested. What remains is for you to believe and seek God.

The hunger of our Lord Jesus Christ is a vital component of the Great Lent. Had this not been mentioned in the Gospel, the total abstinence would not be a practice. Physical hunger is a component of fasting. Jesus spoke of the hunger whose physical appearance translates into a Spiritual Hunger and Thirst and Jesus blessed this type of yearning, "Blessed are those who hunger and thirst for righteousness, for they will be filled." (Matt 5:6) As the ultimate goal is to be filled with the grace of our Lord.

After fasting for forty days, he was hungry. The word "hungry" is very significant; it explains the whole concept of fasting; it reveals the mystery of the Lord's gift when he was on the cross; his body was thirsty for water, by the same token, his spirit also thirsted for souls to seek salvation. I also wish to add and confirm in our minds that we are members of Christ's body, all what takes place in Christ's body, takes place in ours.

For this reason, it is important that when we fast the holy forty days, the whole church participates. One may argue "this is a personal choice". Fair enough, but we are all members of the one body and members must share the same feeling. The LORD hungered and the whole church is yearning for Jesus.

Fasting and retreat: At the end of Christ's fasting for forty days

These forty days were also part of Christ's private life; for him the forty day retreat and fasting were linked. This was an exit from the world and retreat on the mountain.

Therefore, our church places great significance on this practice during this period of fasting. Whereby a retreat is part and parcel of the Great Lent, to a degree where we must try to retreat from socialising, technology and constant communication with others, from shallow reading and from other distractions. In other words, retreating during Lent does not mean from hunger only, because when Jesus began fasting He left for the wilderness. Otherwise He could have completed His fasting in the Temple among people.

Fasting seems to be a hard task when one begins, yet and as you progress it becomes a spiritual peace, which is possible only through being in the sole company of God. A retreat in the company of God may be in the wilderness, in the bedroom, in a room, alone, etc.

When fasting was mentioned in the Old Testament, it was combined with a retreat. "Declare a holy fast; call a sacred assembly. Summon the elders and all who live in the land to the house of the Lord your God, and cry out to the Lord." (Joel 1:14)

When our Lord retreated it was for us to follow His example. Retreat is not detachment; rather it is to be filled with the Holy Spirit, away from the hustle and bustle and returning to cope through the strength of the Holy Spirit.

The sequence of the Great Lent could not have been random:

1. Retreat

2. Fast

3. Hunger

4. Temptation

Clearly this is the sequence followed by the Church who is a member in the body of Jesus Christ, we practise what He has been through.

Another factor is, whoever walks down this path and does so alongside Jesus whose fasting is combined with our own weak fasting, the whole church as a member of Christ's body goes through the Great Lent in unison, in body and spirit, in true dedication. Christ, as the Head of the Church, leads us through the fast, and whoever misses the procession, loses the benefit.

The Temptation

Now we come to the Temptation - which is the subject of our current discussion and which we cannot separate from the sequence, as previously mentioned.

Did Satan go to tempt Jesus? No. It was in fact Jesus who went to be tempted by Satan, which is a totally different situation. A caveat here, it is not right for anyone of us to go to be tempted by Satan.

However, it is possible for Jesus to do so because Satan has no power over Jesus. Satan is helpless before Jesus, who is sinless and has no weaknesses. For this reason, Satan would not dare to go near Him; it was He who went to him. So why did Jesus do this?

Let this point be clear in your minds: Christ is the Head of the Church. He was not tempted for His own person, because Satan is nothing before Him. He was tempted on our behalf and Jesus triumphed on our behalf. He led us through this fierce war by which He demonstrated His full authority over Satan through this great victory. He, once and for all, concluded this old enmity between Him and the human race when Adam was sent away from Paradise and Satan gloated over this defeat, considering it as his own victory over the human race.

Why did Christ become incarnate?

For this reason He was incarnated and became our brother. He became the same in terms of flesh and blood, and on our behalf He removed our shame. On our behalf He was tempted, He fought our battles and on our behalf He triumphed. I repeat He was incarnated because Jesus Christ is the Head of the Church, and because we are all a part of is His Holy body.

The Triumph

The Lord's triumph over Satan is a triumph for all of us. From a theological perspective this is very profound to fathom. In respect to Christianity, a triumph is not an anticipated future occurrence. It has already occurred in the past because the enemy with whom we are dealing, who is Satan, was actually defeated.

To be clear, Satan has already been defeated. One may argue that it may be so that Satan has not yet been defeated. However these days, some people go through hell because of Satan. My response is that some people suffer and go through hell by their own choice. Satan has nothing to do with this. It is because of their own worldly inclinations and concerns that they walk to him (that is, Satan) by choice, and Satan puts them through hell. Never, ever can Satan overpower God's children. The 'triumph' which we are discussing, is not a future one. Our situation versus Satan has already been determined. It has already taken place and had been concluded at the temptation on the mountain.

Is the 'Triumphant Church' only in Heaven?

Some call our church on earth 'The Militant Church' and the one in Heaven 'The Triumphant Church'. I wish to clarify that Christ's triumph over the temptation is a triumph for the whole church. For this reason I wish we call our church 'The Triumphant Church'. This expression came to us from the West. We should always refer to the Earthly Church as a Triumphant Church, and the same for the Church in Heaven. One may refer to the church on earth as 'The Church in Diaspora' because it is still on a journey in a foreign land, and the one in Heaven is the 'Church in Homeland', meaning the Church that has returned from the journey safely.

We should call the church on earth "The Triumphant Church" because the Head (Jesus Christ) triumphed and this is now an accomplished fact. We are enjoying and living in the fullness of that triumph. One may say to me "Father, sometimes we suffer serious falls" and I answer that with "Don't worry, our Head triumphed, He lifts you up."

The cause of our weaknesses

The cause of our weakness is often our own fault, because if we are aware of the strength of the infinite power inherent within us, which is the power of our Lord Jesus Christ, the Christian Church of Martyrs would have lived the fullness of triumph. We are not supposed to lead a life beneath that of the Church of Martyrs, the 'Persecuted Church'.

Referring to persecution it was not like the persecution of the modern era. Persecution was ruthless, but the Church remained solid and triumphant with her head raised.

Characteristic of our Church

The Church was a Prayerful Church, a Church of Worship. We were told that the Monks could be heard across the desert chanting like the cooing of doves. Family life was a perfect representation of Christian life. When one visited any Christian home, there was always a Prayer Corner, with children reciting the Psalms, chantings continued all day. If you visited farms, children were sowing and chanting hymns.

The Church has lived a constant triumph. I do not wish to define it as a Triumphant Church, because she will have this definition in Heaven. We are the Triumphant Church; true in a foreign land but we are crossing over through a diaspora, nevertheless, triumphantly. If asked why do I say so? I say "Why not? With the Church Head being The Lord Jesus, He triumphed over Satan through the Temptation, He crushed him when He was on the cross, He crushed death with His own death, and He sentenced sin through his sinless body. In all directions He fought and He was triumphant. He carried the burden of all our sins on the wooden cross."

This is our Christ. I do not wish to move a step during the Great Lent without HIM being on my side. He is my Head, He is the Head of the Church.

Please, do not fast nor strive to fast unless you realize

that you are a member of the body of Christ, once you have realised this only then should you fast and strive. This is when you will find everything paved before you and you will enjoy the sweet taste of closeness to Jesus.

Is Fasting a Burden?

When does fasting turn into a burden, temptation becoming a burden, with fear and terror of Satan? It is when I am immersed in my individuality: my aloneness.

The Church is defined as being 'The Congregation of the Faithful' which, in my opinion, is very deficient, because people can congregate anywhere. The Church is actually the membership of the body of Christ as we have one Father, one Mother, one Baptism, one Spirit (not two), and one Sacramental Body which we all share in Communion.

When I was young, about 15 years ago, I was still a novice in priesthood I learnt a lesson. Among the congregation, there was a young man (may he rest in pease) who was truly devout. When he came for confession, he mentioned some grave sins, not typical of him. I could not believe that he committed those sins, and I thought that perhaps he had led a double life. Nevertheless, I could not attribute those sins to him. At the end of each confession, he sobbed and said "Father, punish me or give me some kind of disciplinary penance for my sins". One day, I could not help it and I asked him "You are a role model in church, what is it that leads you to this path?" He answered "Father, I share an apartment with a Christian young man, and these are his sins. Aren't we one in the body of Christ? Doesn't his sin hurt Christ and so does mine?" I thought to myself "this is the sense of oneness in Christ". This was the sublimity of spirituality that this young man had reached, and it is with this feeling we should fast.

It is with such a feeling we go through temptation, we tolerate each others weaknesses and it is with such a feeling that the sin of each church member, regardless of its seriousness, is also ours. What is the difference? Christ is one not two - had this been the case, we would have been like the elder son when he spoke to his father "I didn't do anything wrong, it is this prodigal son of yours who is a scoundrel. I have always been your obedient son". Thus, the church throughout its disciplines of fasting, confession, penance, suffering, and also in our sins, the Church is one. If our sins are placed as the sacrifice, what difference does it make whether it is your sin or mine?

The True Christian

In order to be a true Christian, I should share the feelings of each Church member. When a brother commits a sin, it is as if it is I who commit the sin. It is my sin because we are two arms within the same body. When we take the step towards fasting, we should move with the same enthusiasm. We lead the same triumphant life as one solid triumphant church.

The Temptations

Jesus, who is our Head, went out to be tempted by Satan who tempted Him three times. These have been described by the Apostle "For all that is in the world—the lust of the flesh, the lust of the eyes, and the pride of life—is not of the Father but is of the world" (1 John 2:16) and I believe these three are:

• The first: Hunger

"If you are the Son of God, command these stones to become loaves of bread."

• The second: The Ego

"If you are the Son of God, throw yourself down"

• The third: Glory

"All these I will give you"

These were the three temptations in an attempt to lure Jesus by Satan. Now, why three? Here, I want you to pause a moment. Believe me, if you study these three temptations in depth, you will find that you covered all areas of Satan's wars waged against us, because this temptation was not something that happened by chance along the way. No, it was well calculated similar to a set programme: the lust of the flesh, the lust of the eyes, and the pride of life. I will refer to these again later.

Let us start with the lust of the flesh: the bread. Satan told Jesus "If you are the Son of God, command these stones to become loaves of bread." Our Lord answered "'Man shall not live by bread alone, but by every word that comes from the mouth of God.'" The Word is Christ. He wanted to tell foolish Satan "I am Christ, the word of God." In other words, "Man shall not live by bread alone, but by Christ the WORD of God."

The Temptation, why was it in the form of bread? That is because it is a staple food. Starting from childhood, through to old age, we eat bread. Traditionally, it is bread for breakfast, for lunch or for dinner. Whether one is poor or rich, sick or healthy, we all eat bread, it is even a metaphor for living "bread winner".

Christ tells us that is He is our daily bread, our life. Your bread was a seed buried in the ground, it became a plant producing wheat, which was milled and Jesus gave it to you.

Bread does not give the 'Life'

I want you to remember while you are eating your loaf of bread that bread, as a substance, does not give life. It is God within the bread that does. For this reason, I pray during meals because so when I eat, I feel that I am having this morsel from God's hand. One labours the whole day and with the sweat of one's brow to earn the living which colloquially is called the morsel of bread (all day chasing the morsel of bread.)

The first temptation was the bread, the sustenance of beings. Before the fall, Adam's life was not independent of God. He felt His presence all the time, heard His voice in the morning breeze, was in His company through the day. At night he looked forward to hearing His voice again through the breeze. His main sustenance was being in God's presence. Something similar to our daily sustenance on this earth is reading the Gospel, which is a truly great practice, read a verse and reflect on it. Try this practice, it may be a simple verse, but it may give you the motivation to continue and move forward. This verse may be more nourishing than the loaf of bread and may keep you going the whole day.

During this materialistic era which we are living now, bread is a major problem for the world and although there are famines, in some countries there is a superfluous amount of food and people are always satisfied. However, those who live in affluence have other serious problems: ordeals, illnesses, worries, etc and having bread for them is not considered such a big issue, because bread does not solve these issues.

We have the parable of the rich man who stacked his warehouses thinking that he would live forever and he said to himself, 'This is what I'll do. I will tear down my barns and build bigger ones, and there I will store my surplus grain. And I'll say to myself, "You have plenty of grain laid up for many years. Take life easy; eat, drink and be merry." But God said to him, 'You fool! This very night your life will be demanded from you. Then who will get what you have prepared for yourself?' (Luke 12:16-17)

Christ's comment on this parable was along these lines of 'Listen to me, you don't understand me properly because you are unable to realize that I am the Head of the Church and you are members of the Church Body. I am the vine and you are the branches." Where else will

Life come from?"

Manna

In the Old Testament, Manna was miraculously sent as food from Heaven for the Israelites in the wilderness; it was kneaded and baked in Heaven, and Jesus said to them,

"Very truly I tell you, it is not Moses who has given you the bread from heaven, but it is my Father who gives you the true bread from heaven. For the bread of God is the bread that comes down from heaven and gives life to the world."...."I am the bread of life. Whoever comes to me will never go hungry, and whoever believes in me will never be thirsty... I am the bread of life. Your ancestors ate the manna in the wilderness, yet they died. But here is the bread that comes down from heaven, which anyone may eat and not die. I am the living bread that came down from heaven. Whoever eats this bread will live forever. This bread is my flesh, which I will give for the life of the world... Very truly I tell you, unless you eat the flesh of the Son of Man and drink his blood, you have no life in you. Whoever eats my flesh and drinks my blood has eternal life, and I will raise them up at the last day. For my flesh is real food and my blood is real drink. Whoever eats my flesh and drinks my blood remains in me, and I in them. Just as the living Father sent me and I live because of the Father, so the one who feeds on me will live because of me. This is the bread that came down from heaven. Your ancestors ate manna and died, but whoever feeds on this bread will live forever."

Blessed is he who embraces Christ as his own life. Jesus says "he will live forever". Reflect on the peace that you will enjoy after participating in the Holy Sacrament.

Sequence

The temptation on the mountain, fasting, hunger, craving and then eating and drinking the body and blood of the Lord is the triumph. For this reason during days outside Lent, we fast nine hours before the communion, or begin the fast from midnight.

Why do we do this? It is so that we are able to walk the same steps which Christ had walked. He fasted, He experienced hunger, He was tempted, "command these stones to become loaves of bread" by which The Lord answered "Man shall not live by bread alone, but by every word that comes from the mouth of God.'" Where is the Word of God in the altar? It is present through His body and blood, being His sacrifice for our sake.

The bread was first temptation being the temptation for all of us, which Daniel also experienced when he told the King to test him for ten days, since the king wishes to place his neck under the sword. The king replied that Daniel must eat and drink well. Daniel told him that if they were to test him, that life is not all about the King's food and wine, nor is it about anything else, and asked the King to provide him with fruits, vegetables and legumes.

At the end of the ten days Daniel's countenance looked healthier than any of those who were with him. God also blessed him with a sound mind and wisdom far better than any of the profoundly wise men of his time. He was an example of one who lived through the grace of our Lord.

How does the Church continue to exist?

The experience of the Church today is that she lives towards eternal life through Christ. Not dependent on bread alone. The church is blessed through means of its support: her endowments, her finances, and her assets, and as members of the Church body, our life also rotates around this point. However, if a Christian reached the point of realizing that our life is actually a gift from God who is the One who gives the health and the power, then one becomes like Daniel, living by the Word of God.

In real life, if a child does not eat in the morning and again not at lunch, parents worry greatly. However, if the child does not read the Gospel, or does not memorize a verse or two and does not keep reflecting on any verse, this is not a cause of concern. So what?

The parents main concern is focused on giving the child the physical sustenance. Let your main concern be the spiritual sustenance. Give your child the spiritual life.

During this present day and age our main concern revolves around our physical needs more than on our spiritual needs. For example, we are constantly worried about food, clothing, etc. We may even call this era 'The Physical Needs Era'. It has reached a stage where if you have money in your pocket, you are not. No. This mustn't be so, my friends, we should still maintain that our lives rest between the palms of God and that "Man shall not live by bread alone, but by every word that comes from the mouth of God."

Now, I will refer to the second temptation and at the sam time try to show the connection between it and the first one.

The Second Temptation

"Then the devil took him to the holy city and set him on the pinnacle of the temple and said to him, 'If you are the Son of God, throw yourself down....' and in the first temptation, "The devil said to him, "If you are the Son of God, tell this stone to become bread."

Can you notice the same prelude to each temptation? "If you are the Son of God..." Here, the war is one of creating doubt. It is a psychological war; Satan wanted our Lord to doubt his Filiality of God His Father. It is the very same war that is waged against us. He wants us to doubt our Filiality of our Heavenly Father; but no, we are standing on solid grounds we are supported by our firm belief, we call Him "Abba, our Father."

The Heavenly Father

We pray daily "Our Father..." and in our daily life, we also are regularly tested by Satan. Torturing us with whisperings such as: "Let us see how far this person whom you call your 'Heavenly Father' will be able to help you. Place before Him your needs and let us see how far will he be able to fulfil them. Is He actually a Heavenly Father or mere talk? If He is truly a Heavenly Father He will make life easy for you". There are so many 'ifs'.

Believe me my children there is no one among us, including our church, against whom Satan does not wage his wars. I know the Lord's Prayer is often recited repeatedly, without reflecting on its spiritual depth. Nevertheless our Christianity rotates around the fact that God is our Father. Pray in your bedroom, talk to your Father. When you fast, no one has to know, same with charity, because your Father is the one who knows. "You therefore must be perfect, as your heavenly Father is perfect." (Matt 5:48) You were not given a spirit of servitude, rather you were blessed with the spirit of Filiality. The lack of faith or the lukewarm attitude is mainly due to Satan's war of doubt, regardless of his awareness of the Lord's vigilance and bountiful generosity.

It is on the basis of doubt that Satan is waging his war against Christ, it is the war of spreading doubt. This started with Eve "Now the serpent was more crafty than any of the wild animals the Lord God had made. He said to the woman, "Did God really say, 'You must not eat from any tree in the garden'?" This was Satan's deceitful rephrasing of God's command to Adam and Eve "any tree". He did that to portray God's image to Eve as being oppressively cruel, while in actuality that God's fatherly love was, is and will always be the same. For this is what the Lord Almighty says: "...for whoever touches you touches the apple of his eye." (Zech 2:8)

Also, God's ultimate love "For God so loved the world that he gave his one and only Son, that whoever believes in him shall not perish but have eternal life" (John 3:16). Our Lord's paternal love of the human race is limitless and should never be subject to doubt.

During the previous chapters, we covered the subject of God's Fatherhood. The main asset, rather the prime asset of Christianity is that we have a Heavenly Father, who is loving, mighty, protective, generous and leading, even though in most cases we are mean and ungrateful.

Our Heavenly Father's open arms are there for us at all times, where there is sin, there is mercy and forgiveness: "His left arm is under my head and his right arm embraces me." (Song of Solomon 2:6)

That was how our saintly forefathers lived. They enjoyed the perfect paternity of God. This was how the Church always lived, I do not wish to use the similarity used by Jesus "as a hen does gather her brood under her wings" (Luke 13:34; Matt 23:37) because I prefer to use this strong example when He said "I bare you on eagles' wings, and brought you unto myself." (Exodus 19:4) In simple language God is saying to us, that He carried us on His wings and flew us away from the snares of

Satan and into His Fatherly embrace. This is a stronger statement, which we should bear in mind when we are battling against the doubts which Satan tries hard to instil within us. "See what great love the Father has lavished on us, that we should be called children of God!" (1 John 3:1)

We need to pause at a vitally important point which occupies our thoughts: without a doubt we are God's children, but how is it that God allows doubt find its way to us? Being God's children, we must be in God's image: "That which is born of the flesh is flesh; and that which is born of the Spirit is spirit." (John 3:6) The Word became flesh and dwelt amongst us.

It is true, that in spite of the fact of our being God's children, doubts find its way to our minds. However, by the same token, God gave us the strength and Grace to overcome these weaknesses. Jesus is the Son of God by nature, we are God's children by adoption: "Father, I want those you have given me to be with me where I am, and to see my glory, the glory you have given me because you loved me before the creation of the world." (John 17:24)

While we are on the journey of our Great Lent, let us walk through the path of temptation with confidence that we are in the bosom of our Heavenly Father, believing that our whole life rests between the palms of His hands and ultimately when we leave, our departure will be triumphant.

Going back to the two temptations, in one of them Satan tempted the Lord to throw Himself from the pinnacle of the Temple. This is because there is a tradition in the Jewish Talmud which states Christ's second coming will be on the pinnacle of the Temple. Satan is wicked he knows very well that Christ knows what is in the Talmud; that is why he told him to go and throw himself from the pinnacle of the Temple.

Satan thought of tempting the Lord, with the average human lure, for instance the trap of grandeur. He even went to the extent of telling him not to worry because when he throws himself, as no harm will befall him because the angels will attend to him.

Christianity believes in absolute humility. So why should I throw myself from high? For what purpose should I go through this acrobatic dive? Nowhere in the Holy Bible there is such irrational behaviour. When Jesus saw anyone in hardship he never hesitated to help. He could not help himself when He saw the widow of Nain grieving for her son, he asked those who carried the coffin to stop, he touched the coffin and the widow's son arose. When He saw that the multitudes were hungry, He fed them. All of the miracles performed by Jesus were mixed with His tender love.

Nothing could hurt our church grater than trying to attract attention. Our church bears in mind the saying of "shade your candle from the wind, it will remain lit". The Copts have always been quiet worshippers and their relationship with God had always been private. Their private prayers in their own rooms shook strongholds of devils; "All glorious is the princess within her chamber". (Psalm 45:13) This has always been their way - in private and in humility. Some thought that they could not stand in the face of persecution, they were ridiculed but they were solid similar to the Psalmist David when he was a boy who stood before the fearsome Goliath.

Third Temptation

The third temptation of Satan where he was offering all the kingdoms on earth.

How could Satan offer this? That is why Satan also bears the name 'The king of liars': "for he is a liar and the father of lies." (John 8:44) This has always been his method of temptation; through the lust of the eyes, which is the trap up to this very moment and the problem of all times. Someone coveting the home of his neighbour, a girl covets the dress of her friend. Always coveting what we do not have or own.

What a fool the Devil is. Doesn't Satan know that Jesus came here as a King to reign over His own Kingdom. Some people are still talking about an earthly kingdom. The Jews are still waiting for the coming of the Messiah, while the Messiah had already come and saved us and reigned.

"And I, if I be lifted up from the earth, will draw all men unto me." (John 12:32) He has already lifted us; when He reigned on the wooden cross and later when He was finally lifted to Heaven. Christ reigned over the hearts of all of us. Who can ever give up Christ, even if offered all earthly kingdoms?

Once more, the need to emphasize the temptation through the lust of the eye: "The eye is the lamp of the body. If your eyes are healthy, your whole body will be full of light. But if your eyes are unhealthy, your whole body will be full of darkness. If then the light within you is darkness, how great is that darkness!" (Matt 6:22)

The lusting of the eye is insatiable. We pray the Lord to save us from being envious, lustful or covetous because if we follow our own desires we will be like the book of Ecclesiastes description "All streams flow into the sea, yet the sea is never full...The eye never has enough of seeing, nor the ear its fill of hearing." (Ecclesiastes 1:1-8)

I do not wish to elaborate further on the temptation of doubt; in addition to other tests of endurance, for example persecution, or creating problems within Churches. Or even testing us through lusting for grandeur in the form of desires for opulence such as the latest fashions or cars, etc, and several other temptations. Satan's tests are various and systematic.

One of our forefathers described the eyes as being similar to a camera and when we see, the images become inverted, and these are processed in our sub-conscious, and translated in our desires.

Satan was defeated more than once, because Jesus exposed the tactics of the war he wishes to wage over us and showed us the means of self-defence. Christ became our Custodian: He tells us that we are the sheep of His pasture and that He is the Head of the Church. We need to persevere through fast and prayer, and to live for Him and be triumphant in His name.

Jesus showed us all of Satan's tactics to defeat the human race and nothing was concealed. We know everything about Satan. Through Jesus, we also know that Satan is persistent, he never gives up and that he

Satan hid himself in Peter's words:

"From that time on Jesus began to explain to his disciples that he must go to Jerusalem and suffer many things at the hands of the elders, the chief priests and the teachers of the law, and that he must be killed and on the third day be raised to life. Peter took him aside and began to rebuke him. "Never, Lord!" he said. "This shall never happen to you!" Jesus turned and said to Peter, "Get behind me, Satan! You are a stumbling block to me; you do not have in mind the concerns of God, but merely human concerns."

Thus, Jesus exposed to us all Satan's tactics and we are triumphant in His Name.

The Prodigal Son

The Fourth Sunday of the Holy Great Lent

This Sunday falls in the middle of the Great Lent journey so to enable us to empathise with the situation of the Prodigal Son's, although some have instead referred to his as the 'Smart Son'. Rather than thinking that you would never behave in such a manner as the Prodigal Son, it is not a bad idea to place ourselves in his shoes. The Holy Gospel tells us to "Consider the outcome of their way of life and imitate their faith." Ultimately what matters is that the son returned to the Father's bosom, and is the epitome among the parables that our Lord Jesus Christ spoke about repentance.

There were many other parables describing spiritual fervency, enthusiasm and determination. As examples of clear spiritual fervency we have:

• The Samaritan woman: who bravely left her water jar behind together with all her past and began a new start;

• The thief on the cross: a brave man, where during his last and worst moment he said loudly "Jesus, remember me when you come into your kingdom."

We have the Book of Revelation where the first, second and third chapters speak about the seven epistles sent to the seven churches, all of them calling for repentance or reproaching them for losing their spiritual fervency, love and becoming lukewarm. St John wrote:

• "Yet I hold this against you: You have forsaken the love you had at first";

• "Remember therefore from where you have fallen; repent...";

• "You say, 'I am rich; I have acquired wealth and do not need a thing.' But you do not realize that you are wretched, pitiful, poor, blind and naked."

This is a great tragedy that you say you are rich and that you in want of nothing. Therefore, it becomes apparent that you are drowning in compounded sin; you are not aware that you are wretched, poor, blind and naked. In another instance he says: "So then because you are lukewarm, and neither cold nor hot, I will spew you out of my mouth." (Rev 3:16)

A common factor in all the examples and parables about repentance is fervency. I want to focus on this point and draw my own present day parallels in respect of our spiritual regress. We are becoming lax, for example, personally I became used to the fact that every Friday and Sunday I go to Church, I pray the liturgy while standing before the altar. The whole process became a routine, then I was awakened by the reproach through the following passage "Yet I hold this against you: You have forsaken the love you had at first", the voice continues to enquire where my love that I held in my heart when I previously stood before the altar, with my eyes full of tears, when I was compelled by spiritual fervency.

It is a common complaint and we often ask ourselves 'what is happening to us?' At first when we came to Church our hearts were open and receptive. Did our frequent attendance at church and listening to God's word constantly cause us to become lukewarm? "I remember the days of long ago; I meditate on all

your works and consider what your hands have done."
(Psalms 143:5)

These were wonderful days, and spiritually nurturing.
That is why we are reminded to return to the love we
had at first and to "Remember therefore from where you
have fallen; repent."

I remember my first confession, it was warm and sincere.
Then, my life became monotonous and confession
became a routine. The first sacrament had a powerful
impact, I felt that God came into my life and that I did
actually receive Christ's body and blood.

Is repentance confined only to restraining oneself
from stealing, lying and from any evil act? No. We are
constantly reminded to remember our first love. Try to
trace where the love you had at first had gone because
now, right from the start our repentance is lukewarm, very
lukewarm, with no effort, fervency or enthusiasm. The
whole thing passes as if it has never happened. Excuses
follow such as that you have previously confessed these
sins, why should I go and repeat the same. You return to
confession with a lukewarm heart, thinking that simply
listing your sins before your confession father is enough.

Repentance

Briefly, the repentance of all the people mentioned in this and other sermons, was distinctive by their determination, their spiritual fervency, and their overflowing love of our Lord, their determination never to sin anymore.

The life of the Samaritan woman changed completely. It was a similar to the Prodigal Son: it was not possible for him to repent while he continued living where he was. He had to leave in order to return to his Father's embrace. There was no way for him to continue living with swines in an unreachable country.

Without detaching from sin, repentance is futile. Zacchaeus had to detach himself from his Tax Collector's Desk. He sincerely repented and returned to the people fourfold what he had collected from them. Repentance has a clear-cut line between the past and whatever evil was committed, and the new life.

My brethren, repentance is vital for a Christian who needs to build one's life on a solid foundation, and cannot be cold or lukewarm. "I know your deeds, that you are neither cold nor hot. I wish you were either one or the other! So, because you are lukewarm—neither hot nor cold - I am about to spit you out of my mouth."

(Rev 3:16) Many things in our life need to be excised for our repentance to be effective.

Repentance must be sincere and heartfelt.

If I have no forgiveness within my heart, I need to train myself to forgive, and this has already been discussed: "..and forgive us our trespass, as we forgive those who trespassed against us..." Our Lord tells us that repentance includes many factors related to our heart, and if when we fast, we must be particular about what goes through our mouths. He tells us that this should not be our main concern, because it is what comes out of our mouths that we should be concerned about.

We are not like the literal people who pick and choose whatever suits their own purpose. When it comes to the Gospel we take it as a whole. True, when Jesus fasted He abstained from food, but at the same time He taught us that fasting is also with the heart and with what comes from our hearts through our mouths "A good man brings good things out of the good stored up in his heart, and an evil man brings evil things out of the evil stored up in his heart. For the mouth speaks what the heart is full of." (Luke 6:54)

Human beings are strange creatures, they can harbour strange thoughts within their minds, for example: hatred, grudges, adultery, lewdness, stealing, etc. While we speak about love during Lent we also harbour hatred, and he who hates one's brother commits murder. In our hearts we commit stealing. One could question whether it is truly possible to commit the sin of stealing within your own heart. Yes, you can. Stealing does not have to be the physical act. When you covet another's property and wish if you can steal it, this is actually stealing.

St Mark mentions also that thoughts of blasphemy add arrogance and envy.

All these are thoughts that emanate from the heart. Jesus wants to demonstrate to us that while we fast we become scrupulous about what we eat, at the same time we need to watch what comes out of the mouth, because through the mouth we receive the body and blood of our Lord, and whoever receives this sacrament is to utter what glorifies and praises the name of our Lord. The heart is the centre. These are very important concepts for repentance.

Figuratively speaking, repentance involves a severing action, once and for all separating one life and another. It has to be fervent and strong, not lukewarm. This applies to the genuine penitent. As to the lukewarm penitent, who are on and off, these will never repent.

Another aspect is that penitence has to be sincere, coming out of one's heart. One has to scrutinize one's heart starting from the innermost and to deeply examine it: is it envy or evil thoughts or murder or arrogance? Is it blasphemy? Stealing? Where do I start? Start from the heart as chapter fifteen in the Gospel of St Luke fully explains.

The Son and the Steward

As mentioned earlier, repentance has a totally different meaning for us Christians.

The prodigal son returned to his father's bosom and when he did so, he did not start by saying straight away "Now I'll go back to my father". No. It was after he reflected:

"But when he came to himself, he said, 'How many of my father's hired servants have bread enough and to spare, and I perish with hunger! I will arise and go to my father, and will say to him, "Father, I have sinned against heaven and before you, and I am no longer worthy to be called your son. Make me like one of your hired servants."'

One of the prodigal son's friends might have mentioned to him that it would be better to work as a hired servant in the house of his father, as opposed to the house of another and it would be a better situation for him. But it was a call within himself telling him to return to his father, even as a servant: being a servant with his father was better than being a servant with anyone else. It was like a hidden tie, like an umbilical cord. This is the filial tie, which is mutual: a father cannot sever it, nor can a son. It was because of this Filiality the son, after reflection, said to himself: "I will arise and go to my father, and will say to him, "Father, I have sinned against heaven and before you, and I am no longer worthy to be called your son. Make me like one of your hired servants."

In our Church, repentance starts with the Baptism. It is the sacrament whereby we become God's children, when we start calling Him "Our Father, who are in Heaven..." Our Abba. In order to bring this concept closer to your mind, I want you to draw a simple comparison between the way you treat your son within your own home. You do not treat him like a hired servant when he does a good job, you tell him "Here is your pay, go for a walk down the street and do whatever you wish". You treat him on the basis that you love him, and because you love him, you discipline him often. You do not do this with a paid servant, where your relationship ends at the end of the working day. The relationship which begins at our baptism is the umbilical cord which ties us to our Father, it is the blessing towards our repentance in future, giving it a totally different concept.

During sermons, preachers speak about sins and their variety: murder, stealing, and other sins, in addition to thoughts and only God knows what goes on within the human mind. When talking about adultery, our Preacher Apostle Paul sums it up "Therefore whoever disregards this, disregards not man but God, who gives his Holy Spirit to you."

Repentance in Christianity

Sin began to take a different meaning in Christianity. The Apostle Paul says: "For we are members of his body, of his flesh, and of his bones." Is it possible to involve members of Christ's body in sin? This concept is different to our understanding; it does not mean only a transgression against someone, and that is where it ends. The sin is directed at God the Father Himself.

In terms of committing a sin, a person goes through two stages. In the first stage, a person may not be aware that by sinning, the sin is directed at God Himself and once he realizes that, he says to himself that he will never do it again because he realizes the extent of God's love towards him, "I will not cause Jesus further suffering" because no one other than Christ carries our sins "Surely

He has borne our grief and carried our sorrows". We detest sin, nevertheless we fall in its trap. Now, the person develops a different attitude, realising that as much as they love the Lord, they should detest sin. Never return to it, nor immersed in worldly lures again. Not to return God's love with ingratitude and sin again.

It would be similar to the Prodigal Son's reaction if his friends returned to him to go back to his previous life and the cycle of old sins, by asking him to rejoin them. His response would be "I can't hurt my father again. At first I did out of ignorance, I never imagined the extent of his love for me, but now that I know, I can never hurt him again."

Secondly, repentance also means that our Lord rejoices in our return. The Prodigal Son or the "Smart Son" was not the only one who found peace, his father also found peace and rejoiced in embracing him, having him back in his bosom. Repentance is bilateral: peace to the penitent and joy to the recipient.

True repentance means severance of the life of sin, but unfortunately it is a recurring situation. I walk beside the Lord and on the way I see the light which shows me the stains of my sins, and I keep wiping them, each time the light becomes brighter the stains are magnified. For this reason we should not be surprised when we hear or read about saints, we learn that throughout their lives they are constantly in a state of penitence, because it is human nature to sin; there are always certain issues which remain within us some being with our knowledge and others being without our knowledge.

However, through the Lord's grace, each time we become closer to Him, we yearn more and more towards repentance: it is a continuous process. It is not possible that you come one day and say "That's it. I've repented, now I am safe". If you develop this attitude, you will come to a state where nothing has any meaning anymore. You will not enjoy the sacrament on the altar; it becomes tasteless. The absolution given by the priest becomes meaningless. Attending the Liturgy becomes a routine, because you will feel similar to the Pharisee who once said "Thank you Lord because I am not like those others."

It is a fact, for those who are in communion with The Lord through repentance, they become closer and feel their weaknesses even more. Each time they beseech the Lord, praying "O Lord, help me. Strengthen me towards repentance and starting anew."

The history of the Church tells us that St Anthony, that with the dawn of each day, awoke with the following prayer: "Lord, I will begin my new day with you. It is different than the one that has gone, which was not a perfect one. I did not start my first step yet. I will start it with you by my side, the walk is a long one." Each day in his life meant a new day. How beautiful would it be that each day is a new day with genuine repentance, we turn our back towards what had gone and face what is to come.

Repentance rejoices in the Lord and it never ends because it is constant. It is a process similar to the growth of a child who grows and the father watches the growth with great joy. The child grows in knowledge and guidance. The concept of sin is not that it is only an evil act, rather a hurt to our Heavenly Father.

The Parable of the Prodigal Son is vital. It is the core of the Great Lent, because the whole Great Lent rotates around the Filial connection of God and the Baptism. That we are actually God's children.

In the middle of the Great Lent, we come across an example of one of God's children: not a good one; in fact, a very bad one. Nevertheless, we saw what a joy he was to his father when he returned earnestly and spiritually penitent, to start a new life, while he was actually his Father's son long, long before.

Some brethren from other denominations often tell us

that X "was renewed on such and such a day" meaning that he repented on that particular day. Thus, he severed his sinful past, throwing away all the old history. However this is not what we say, we describe it as a genuine repentance, because it will be a continuous process. He will keep repeating his repentance as he goes, each time coming closer and closer to God, feeling the joy of approaching his Father's bosom.

I want to delve even further: let us ask ourselves what is the purpose of our repentance? Let us put aside our own individuality. We wish to bring joy to our Father's heart and would it not be an additional joy if we are joined by more penitents? What if we bring a friend, or two or three, for example a colleague at work or at university or a neighbour who is not close to God and we invite them to attend church even if need be, drag them and through this eventually they repent.

The penitent who tastes God's love wishes to share this joy with everyone. The first verse in Song of Songs says "Take me away with you". It says "take me" using a singular pronoun: "me". It means take me and when others see this, they will all run to follow. This is evidenced in the Gospel, those who repented were followed by multitudes. It is not like someone who establishes a certain religion and wishes to multiply his followers. No, it is not so. Our motive is to bring joy to our Father's heart.

In the case of the elder son, it would not have been so bad had he said "Why should I care. My brother committed these bad things, let him go his own way." However, his reaction was "I didn't do anything bad, I have been serving you for many years, yet you give him the preferential treatment?" What he did not realize that the core issue was the repentance of the young son. Had he repented, this would have placed him at par with his brother.

Our sinning hurts Christ, and we have only one Christ. For this reason, when we pray we say "Our Father who are in Heaven." In addition the Apostle Paul teaches us "Now I rejoice in what I am suffering for you, and I fill up in my flesh what is still lacking in regard to Christ's afflictions, for the sake of his body, which is the church." (Colossians 1:24)

When we begin to realize the depth of repentance and the joy it brings to the heart of our Lord, we like to share this joy with others, we bring our children, our neighbour, our colleagues at work we like to call everyone "Take me away with you—let us hurry!" and all will follow, because each one is precious to the Lord. The one who is lost, is more precious than the 99 present, as in the parable of the lost coin. It was not because the lost coin was worth more in terms of currency; it was because of its loss. In the sight of God it had to be found, and added to others.

This Lent time is the time of repentance for those who are within and those who are outside the church. It is the time for all to rejoice in the embrace of The Lord.

Suggested Prayer: Lord, each moment, at all times, we wish to bring joy to your heart, whether we are in the church or among others. We are at your feet with more and more coming, because you receive all the incoming new souls with open arms. People will understand that the meaning of repentance is much, much broader than what people commonly understand. It is the joy to your and our hearts.

My dear friends, repentance being a constant process, is not meant to be as such for the purpose of making us aware of our weaknesses each time we become closer to God, it is because each time we come closer to God, we experience the extent of his love for us, leading us to increase our love for Him. This is the nature of love - the more you receive, the more you give. This is how we define repentance in our church: a constant process even among the saints.

We taste His love and we reciprocate and we continue through the depth of love. How much? However much that is able to fill the infinite. He loved us to the end. Therefore, when I love, I do so even to the extent of martyrdom, our bodies are sacrifices to The Lord. Repentance is a mysterious sacrament.

The Mystery of Repentance

Repentance is feeling the divine love; and each time you sense its infinity, you keep tasting its sweetness and enjoy its sublimity. Therefore, you begin to detach yourself from your ego. God's Love is a love that immerses the whole world and you realise this with each soul joining in repentance; it is like a collective joy. The Lord earnestly seeks each lost soul and he gave examples in the three parables in chapter fifteen of the Gospel of St Luke:

1. The Lost Sheep;

When he found the lost sheep he rejoiced and carried it on his shoulders saying that angels in Heaven also rejoiced. The angels watch the Lord's children and share in the joy. You see, it is not a joy only for God but also for his angels.

2. The Lost Coin;

In the parable of the Lost Coin, the joy extended to neighbours and friends "Come, share my joy, I found my lost coin".

3. The Prodigal Son.

In each parable The Lord spoke of the joy which followed.

In the parable of the Prodigal Son, when the elder son came from outside and heard the noises of singing and rejoicing, he asked what was happening and informed that his younger brother had returned and they had sacrificed a fatted calf in his honour. When he reproached his father, he told him "Son, we ought to rejoice because your brother was dead and now he is alive, he was lost and now he is found."

Rejoicing and Repentance: Serious concepts in our Christian Faith

The common attitude towards repentance is seeking forgiveness with humility and remorse; but what is the outcome? It is love and joy. That is the reason under the New Testament it says "But when you fast, put oil on your head and wash your face, so that it will not be obvious to others that you are fasting." In other words, walk joyfully among people.

It was entirely the contrary under the Old Testament when Daniel said: "I ate no pleasant food, no meat or wine came into my mouth, nor did I anoint myself at all..."

In the New Testament The Lord says, when you fast, rejoice, anoint your head and let no one know that you are fasting.

Repentance, Divine Love, Joy. This is the Lent under the blessings of Grace.

The Samaritan Woman

The Fourth Sunday of the Great Lent

The conversation of our Lord Jesus Christ with the Samaritan Woman was stimulative and very interesting. The essence of the whole talk was summed up in the testimony of the Samaritans, which followed the conversation between our Lord and the woman, and so we truly know that this is Christ, the Saviour who came to save the whole world. Many Samaritans from that town believed in him because of the woman's testimony, when she preached to them that "He told me all that I ever did." Therefore, when the Samaritans came to him, they asked Him to stay with them, and He stayed there two days."

The salvation of the world is not an easy task. It is true there are many people who do good around the world; they are philanthropists, they lead kingdoms, there are those who rescue many and those who work towards the happiness of humankind. However, Salvation of the world is never an easy task. The Divine Revelation intended to give us an example through the Samaritan Woman in that how God works with the whole world on an individual level.

We always take notice of grand acts which relate to a country, or a kingdom. However, it does not occur to our mind that God works on an individual level within each one of us in order to grant this salvation.

In order that we do not perceive salvation as being a simple issue because people generally believe that since Christ came in order to be crucified; He was crucified, He died and was resurrected after three days, and all was finalized and now everything is easy and simple.

Now, the Divine Revelation gives us the example of a woman of this world with Christ standing before her, spending time and effort to lead her to the blessing of salvation. It is easy to say that this situation was not necessary, since in the first place Christ came for the salvation of the whole world. Our response to this idea would be that people do not accept salvation in their lives easily, even those who know about salvation.

During Christ's discussion with this woman He knew that she had she was knowledgable about the topic of salvation. She confirmed to him that they were awaiting the Messiah, even though there were differences between them in the concept itself "The woman said to Him, "Sir, I perceive that You are a prophet. Our fathers worshiped on this mountain, and you Jews say that in Jerusalem is the place where one ought to worship." Ultimately we are all waiting for the coming of the Messiah, and when He comes He will teach us a great deal.

What is your opinion about this woman? Was she pious or not? Did she know about salvation or not? Of course she knew, but through mere talk. Although the concept of salvation reaching the depth of her heart, it was another issue, another very major issue.

Of course, it goes without saying we all know that Christ came, He died and He redeemed the humankind, and His mighty power could heal a person who had been blind for 38 years, and even resurrect the dead. We saw many miracles that were performed by Jesus, but the incident with the Samaritan woman was unique. In their dialogue, the true desire of what Christ's heart towards her soul was became apparent, and the effort made towards her salvation was obvious.

The way I imagine it, during their meeting at Jacob's well was not their first encounter. It would be that this woman was at the bottom of a well similar to an abyss. At the top of the well He was standing holding a rope and calling saying to her "This rescue is easy. Salvation is at hand; shall I drop the rope?" Truly, the well was so deep that she was in the deepest of the depth of despair, she became adapted to her circumstances and resigned to the situation, waiting for the time life would end, albeit at the bottom of a well. In other words, when Jesus spoke to her, He was not speaking to a normal person. He was talking to a person whom had lost all hope. It took time to convince her and change her feelings.

You see my dear brothers and sisters, when the human being was first created, he was created like the image of God. True, he was created from clay; a mixture of water and dirt. He lived in Paradise, materialistically, eating, drinking, and farming, but there was a tender aspect in the life of this first Adam, in that he heard our Lord's voice with the daily gentle morning breeze: this was his daily banquet which he looked forward to each morning.

The Holy Bible tells us that he used to hear God's voice with the morning breeze. Please pause for a moment at this point - can you tell me, how did he hear God's voice? Did he actually see Him with his own eyes, in order to hear His voice?

The Third Hypostasis of the Trinity is the Holy Spirit, and one cannot see the Holy Spirit. The Holy Spirit has no audible sound. So how did Adam hear Him? Is it possible that the first Adam had an additional sense other than the other senses we have today? Did that additional sense enable him to see and feel the presence of our Lord?

As a matter of fact, in the New Testament, Christ implied that one is able to see our Lord even though not visually. "Blessed are the pure in heart, for they will see God." By contrast, in another instance He said those who have ears but do not hear" even though their ears are capable of hearing any sound. Could it be that their ear drums are receptive to certain sound frequencies? For example, there are some creatures who are capable of hearing a certain sound which the human being is incapable of hearing, because their hearing is geared towards a different sound frequency. What I mean by all this is that perhaps humans lost one of the senses whereby they could sense God's presence, or His voice or interaction. They lost this sense that is commonly referred to as 'spirituality'.

Perhaps following the fall, human beings started being preoccupied by ploughing the soil, rearing children, planning and insuring the future of their family. This was the beginning of the separation from God, losing trust that He will provide and instead trusting in their own ability to live securely, how to insure his life, his health, his family, his house, how to save and how to plan for the future, and this is the slow but steady the descent in the well, like the Samaritan woman. Deep down into the well.

This was the stage at which God started to communicate with the humanity. He began by sending his Prophets: one after the other, to enable people to hear his voice but they were deep, very deep in the well.

Here, I do not mean the Samaritan Woman. Even the disciples when they arrived, they also were in another deep well. They were thinking or whispering amongst themselves that the Lord is talking to a sinful person, let alone a sinful woman, what could be compelling Our Lord to do this? Neither the Gospel nor The Lord commented on this point. The Disciples attempted to change the conversation asking our Lord if He wanted something to eat. He told them that He was not hungry, that He was satisfied. They asked him whether the lady gave him something to eat, or someone else gave him something to eat. He told them that he wanted to talk to them about another type of food. What is that food?

We know only one kind of food, but He told them, "I have food to eat of which you do not know....My food is to do the will of Him who sent me and to finish His work." (John 4:32;34) They could not comprehend what He said. In terms of food, they knew only one fact: the human being has a stomach and eats physically food. Incidentally, everyone talks about the food supply crises and famines. Food has to be provided, once the person eats and the stomach is full, the person is satisfied. If the stomach is empty, the person is hungry. That is all what the person knows about food. Jesus very nearly told them "and this is my problem: I will die on the cross; I will redeem you with my own blood and I will be resurrected - all for your sake". Who would be able to comprehend this? Where is the spiritual sense to accommodate this concept?

During the apparitions of the Virgin in the suburb of Zeitoun in Egypt, we heard so much about happy events there, as at that time I was travelling outside Egypt. Naturally, the Jews do not accept easily the spiritual phenomena. They are after something scientifically tangible. Therefore, they ridiculed the phenomenon; at one time they claimed that it was a Russian phenomenon because during that period Russia had status in Egypt; another time they claimed it was an eastern fraud. However, God always has His own witnesses.

There was a Catholic old man who was researching a particular subject which preoccupied him, similar to someone who reads a book and becomes interested in its subject. He read about the coming of the False Messiah, about when when will this False Messiah come? Whether people believe in such things, etc.

A woman had predicted two events, one of them happened and the other did not. The first prophecy was that President Kennedy would be assassinated and the second was that the False Messiah would come in 1962. When the events of the apparitions were all over the world, I do not know how this man's mind interpreted it that the False Messiah appeared in Egypt in 1962 and by 1968, he had been In Egypt for six years and created a fuss. This man was a millionaire and I personally paid him a visit. He sent a Catholic priest, gave him a lot of money and asked him to go and investigate the False Messiah's arrival in Egypt. The man arrived in Egypt and saw for himself and wrote the most wonderful book that was published on a very wide scale. The book was titled "Our Lady Virgin Mary Returns to Egypt" and in his book he presented his testimony - he never thought of the Virgin nor did he have her in mind. Our God, in His miraculous salvation way was able to convey spirituality to the people who microanalyse everything and who find it hard to accept the fact that the Lady Virgin or saints do have spiritual phenomena within the church.

These days we are in the well of the Samaritan Woman: this well is the one of materialistic living. Watch the difference of thought which took place during the dialogue. She talked about being the offspring of Jacob; Christ talked about Christ/the Messiah. Can you see the vast difference between Jacob and Christ? Even if Jacob was the Patriarch of Forefathers, how could he be compared to Christ? She went on and on, talking about being the offspring of Jacob and blindly clinging to the ancestry, while Christ was talking to her about Heaven and how He came from Heaven. She accepts the fact that she is Jacob's daughter, which for her, is better because Jacob had many children, he had a lot of cattle, he had a well from which the cattle drank and the whole story was good, but Christ who comes from Heaven, he comes with spiritual things only.

The difference between the materialistic life and eternal life is the same one between Jacob and Christ, or between the Samaritan woman who is at the bottom of the well and the one who is at the top of the well.

These days the topic of the difference between materialism and spirituality is a hard one to discuss even within the Church, or within our daily life, or when selecting the Holy Bible readings. We are after topics that match our desire to be assured of financial security and peaceful living. But when it comes to talking about the eternal life, the hereafter, caring for others and Christ being with us and takes care of our earthly concerns and inviting us to reflect on heavenly issues, this is very hard these days.

This is day we must concern ourselves with spiritual matters and our salvation. Not with our material and physical surroundings. Pertaining to the salvation through Christ's blood, His crucifixion, His death on the cross.

We are in a well. A very, very deep well. We ask everything of Christ, except salvation. Who among us can honestly state before our Lord that while in Church their whole thoughts focus on the real salvation: the death of Christ on the cross? Who can say that their thoughts constantly reflect on this scene, never to leave their minds, rather than being preoccupied with earthly materialism?

While I did not say that while Adam was in Paradise he

did not eat or did not lead a happy life. Of course he did but he had a special sense which enabled him to recognize our Lord's voice. He heard him daily with the morning breeze. Where did that sense go? Even within the church our discussions rotate around money: our church revenue is so much, our church expenditure is so much, our church is in debt by so much, foreseen projects are so much, and so on.

Speaking of salvation through Christ's blood, or mentioning spiritual issues are extremely hard, due to the fact that the human spiritual sense started to wane and is close to disappearing. For this reason, I am telling you, salvation is not easy. Often people take this matter quite casually remarking "What is the big deal? Christ came, He died, He redeemed the humankind, He saved us. That's it, end of story."

Salvation is not merely that you and I are redeemed, it is regaining that sense through which we realize what God has given each of us personally. The difference between the water which that woman drank and the water which Christ was going to give her, was that Christ was going to give her the water that came from His side; that was what he was talking about, but she was talking about the earthly water.

There is a difference, my beloved, between the way of

life whereby you keep drinking from the earthly water and the other way of life when you start drinking from Christ's water. Often you feel that spiritual sense when, through a sermon, you taste the sweetness of God's word and you become peacefully content. This is what you call satisfaction. The woman understood that Jesus' thirst was physical when she told him that He did not have a pail and the well was very deep, and he explained to her that their concepts were different - the water He gave was different to her water. His water quenched the spiritual thirst.

His Disciples thought that real food was the one they were about to buy, but he said to them "My food is to do the will of him who sent me and to finish his work." When you achieve that spiritual touch in your life, you constantly aspire to do the will of our Lord according to what you read in your Bible. Then this spiritual tendency begins to grow in your life and within yourself you begin to feel the growth of the ever-present capability of receiving the voice of our Lord within your life. You feel that everything around you is working towards your benefit; it is similar to one whose eyes were covered with a film and now the film is removed, everyone sees things black and you see everything white. Our eyes begin to see and find comfort in seeing and reflecting on the icons of the crucifixion, and other icons of Christ, instead of the past insatiable desire, which Solomon described, of watching worthless scenes.

Also, the enjoyment of listening to materialistic earthly topics switches to a joy in listening to the sweet tunes of the Lord's voice and the reassuring sound of His footsteps next to you. Our ears and eyes now yearn to the heavenly and to the eternal.

Dear friends: when I raise these issues, it is not intended to address other people only. First and foremost I mean myself. We are in a well, an extremely deep well and our perception of Christ and related issues to our salvation are very remote. In today's world, materialism dominates over our lives to a stage where we are losing our sense of seeing salvation through each word spoken by Christ and we can no longer feel his presence among us. Just think about the effort He went through to reach the soul of that woman.

She was a materialistic woman like us. She understood the Law and knew of Jacob and the coming of the Messiah, just like any of us. She was a busy person who would wake up in the morning get the water, bring it home, again get up in the morning, get the water and bring it home. And of course like any of us she had the desires of the flesh and she had been married. The Law allowed her to do so, but she went beyond the Law and she was married and divorced five times.

For Christ to approach someone like her to speak to her about spirituality? Of course she was not receptive He spoke and she counter argued. He spoke to her with authority promising her the quenching water and at last, she asked him to give her that water. He asked her to call her husband because, and hypothetically, if He gave her the water in a pail with holes, it would all be wasted. When He asked her to "Call your husband" it was intended to block all the holes, which would allow sin to enter her life. She had five husbands during her lifetime and the one with whom she lived was not her husband. She was surprised as to how He knew this. It was an intrusion into her private life. Of course He knew and this was the first step towards her salvation.

Christ does not want us to be His employees or under a bond of servitude. Never. He wants us to be happy, to drink from his thirst-quenching water.

The point I wish to impress upon you is that when He gives us His thirst-quenching water, He wants us to have this water in sound vessels, lest the precious water leaks through and is wasted. Our souls should be sinless to receive His blessings. This begins by remorse and confession, thus purifying the soul when receiving the pure water. If you have a problem with confession the priest is always there to help.

Why did Jesus ask her to call her husband? Was she stirred by this request? Perhaps. It was because Christ often helps us eliminate certain sores within us. He touched on an innermost wound that was likely to fester. Now is the time that we purify the contents of our souls to enable us to drink from the thirst-quenching water. We have had our fill of the earthly, unquenching water.

When Jesus Christ started speaking to her about her innermost private life, and for the first time she was embarrassed. As mentioned earlier, this woman was quite versed regarding her faith. She told Jesus that it seemed that He knew the details of her life. He confirmed to her that He did and intended that she would enjoy salvation, but as long as she was so remote and would not confess, she could not enjoy the salvation. Thus, she confessed everything and then He promised her His live-giving water. She turned to him with a question about where they are to worship, at Jacob's well or in Jerusalem and how they should worship.

He turned to her and reminded her that she is concerning herself with earthly matters. For many people, these days worship became mere rituals and movements, "Yet a time is coming and has now come when the true worshipers will worship the Father in the Spirit and in truth, for they are the kind of worshipers the Father seeks. God is spirit, and his worshipers must worship in the Spirit and in truth." (John 4:23-24)

We all know about physical worship, but it is the spiritual worship is the peace of the soul. Sometimes the concept of worship boils down to gestures and bodily movements and it should not be so.

People think that by these movements and gestures they act in humility and a contrite spirit, since we are dust and to dust we shall return. They do not realize that kneeling is a spiritual ritual. It is regrettable that our worship has become ritualistic rather than spiritual, for example every Sunday we attend church as a routine. God wants our worship to be spiritual and emanate from the innermost of our souls. The water He gives us is from the Holy Spirit, we have to prepare the channels for that water to flow within us.

The woman started to emerge from her immersion in the deep well, and breathe in the fragrance of Christ. She asked for further information about the Messiah who was to come from Heaven and other issues she did not know of. Jesus told her that He was the One, He was within the reach of everyone, He came to give happiness to all and that He came for the salvation of all. He also told her that she could not perceive this because there was a veil on her eyes, once this veil was removed she would see clearly. Once this veil of earthly preoccupations was gone she could see clearly and see if that man was like all the men she had met and dealt with in the past.

She experienced the spirituality in Him and a new fulfilling purpose was born within her. This is basically what I wish to explain, that this spiritual sense, through the Grace of God, we seek to be born within us. This sense which is to overcome our materialistic preoccupations to enable us to have a spiritually futuristic focus when we try to look ahead whether on earth or towards our eternity, or in respect of events taking place around us. We become receptive to salvation and can truly say that "Truly, Christ is the Saviour of the world". Therefore, Christ will enter our lives, reign over our hearts as a true Spiritual King where we acknowledge him saying "Our Lord Jesus Christ, here we are in your Kingdom". Then our minds become occupied with the spiritual and will be reflected in our action, our speech and our senses. We will develop caution with respect in the manner we worship, we will try to avoid being in the ambit of materialism: because our church was never materialistic.

During Christ's time, he did not build a church, or an institution. None of these things. His mission was towards the salvation of the human soul. If today we have a beautiful church in which we congregate, it is not meant to distract us from our main target; which is meeting Jesus and being attached to Him.

May our Good Lord pick us up from the well of circumstances we find ourselves in. May we be blessed with a sweet union with Christ, similar to the Samaritan Woman. I ask this through the intercession of our Lady Virgin St Mary.

The Paralytic Man

The Fifth and Penultimate Sunday of the Holy Great Lent

The following Sunday will be the last Sunday of the Great Lent, which is the Baptism Sunday. This is the sequence set by the Church to constantly remind us about God's interaction with mankind. This sequence is stated below:

i. On Preparation Sunday we spoke about "But when you pray, go into your room, close the door and pray to your Father, who is unseen."

ii. Then the following Sunday is about God's loving care for His children and His guidance throughout their path.

iii. Temptation Sunday is about that God will not abandon us, even amidst the most severe of temptations because He is our Father.

iv. Sunday of the Prodigal Son we see our Lord's open embracing arms and His infinite love regardless of the seriousness of the sin.

v. Sunday of the Samaritan Woman is the heated dialogue between the Samaritan Woman and our Lord Jesus, in which He was persistent on recovering her soul from perdition and to replace the water she drank by the life-giving water, leading her to a new life of becoming a new person in Christ as a being created in the image of God.

vi. These two forthcoming Sundays, the Sunday of the Paralytic Man and , you will see the clear picture of the bountiful Grace. The blessing of Bethesda, as we said yesterday, was a symbol of Baptism. Around that pool there was a diversity of invalids: blind, lame and crippled and those with other impediments.

Try to picture it: a pool surrounded by people lying around all who suffer from infirmities and. The blind, yet hopeful, and others who were there because they were hopeful that the angel would come and stir the water, only if each could be the first one to fall or roll, or to be dropped into the pool, similar to a race.

The spiritual motivation here was weak, because the coming of the angel was infrequent and random with no set timetable perhaps once a month, once a week and even when he came, the healing was for one person only and the first to get into the pool.

But in the case of the Baptismal Pool, it is the Spirit of our Lord who attends not an angel; thus there is the presence of the Divine Power. Coming to know Christ is truly an eye opener. Before baptism a person is blind, but why do we consider him blind? Because there are many mysteries which are concealed before baptism, "At that time Jesus said, "I praise you, Father, Lord of heaven and earth, because you have hidden these things from the wise and learned, and revealed them to little children." (Matt 11:25) Similar to all of God's revelations, we cannot understand them through the human mind. God enlightened the Disciples' minds to enable them understand the teachings, otherwise everything would have been like riddles for them. He gave them the Grace of wisdom beyond the wisdom of the knowledgeable - they were blind and now they see.

We were crippled because we walked away from our Lord, but now we walk. The main point here is that the sacrament of baptism is a precious and powerful one. It is the Grace in which we live, it is the seal which confirms our love and the presence of the Holy Spirit within us. "Don't you know that you yourselves are God's temple and that God's Spirit dwells in your midst?"

My main issue is that we all realise this fact, that our Lord's Spirit dwells within us regardless of whether we are young or old, rich or poor, with a status or without. The main thing is that our Lord's Spirit dwells with his infinite Grace within us and within the Church, by the same Grace our impediments no longer impair us.

We shall discuss the personality of the Paralytic Man and the dialogue which took place between him and Christ. This man suffered for 38 years, what would anyone expect of him? Of course, psychologically we could infer that he was a wreck. However, all those people who were around the pool had hope. With the passing of each day the constant hope was perhaps that day would be the day they would be healed. But with the passing of each day, there were additional invalids.

With the spread of the news that there was miraculous healing in the pool of Bethsaida, the crowds joined in around the pool and with the increase of crowds the possibility of healing became slimmer, nevertheless there was hope.

The Lord came to speak with the man about this particular point "Do you wish to be healed?" What a strange question. My response to Christ's question is that it means that whoever wishes to receive from Christ, has to be full of hope and determination. If I am the temple of our Lord's Holy Spirit and the Holy Spirit dwells within me, how is it that there is no change in my life?

Can you hear the voice "Do you wish...?" The Holy Spirit is acting within you; the Lord's body and blood are acting within you asking Do you wish ... a total change in your life? This what the Lord is really asking. This indicates a very serious point and the will is a major factor in our relationship with God. Instead of Grace, God gave us Himself and you have the will, if you wish to receive, you can.

If you wish you can you can breathe without impediment, you can fill your lungs. If your lungs are weak, your breathing is weak and the volume of air you inhale will be limited. If you so wish, it is a possibility. The process is now a matter of will. You may notice that all those who followed Christ, did so out of their own free will; Christ did not force them and when they spoke to Christ it was with deep reverence.

Let us return to the conversation with the Samaritan Woman. He asked her for water for him to drink, and also offered her water for her to drink. He spoke to her on the same level. a one-to-one basis. He did not lose His temper nor did he exploit His authority. He spoke to her, rationally and calmly, waiting for her request to giver her the water of which he spoke of, the life-giving water. All you need is your will to ask to as the Lord to give you the same and He will give you. Seek him and ask of Him "Lord, I want to be healed" this is all what He wants to hear from you because we are all suffering from spiritual paralysis

Do you wish to let go of earthly possessions and follow Christ? There was a mention of someone who "went out sad because he had great wealth..."(Matt 19:22; Mark 10:22)

When Christ asked Zacchaeus to hurry and come down, do you think that had Zacchaeus said that he would not come down? Would Our Lord have left him? Even towards His crucifixion, Christ said "Jerusalem, Jerusalem, you who kill the prophets and stone those sent to you, how often I have longed to gather your children together, as a hen gathers her chicks under her wings, and you were not willing. Look, your house is left to you desolate."

(Matt 23:37; Luke 13:34) This will be the Gospel Reading on the last Friday of the Great Lent before Good Friday. This verse makes it clear that the will has to be there. Someone may raise the question that if it is God's will, who can go against it? In answer I say that God greatly respects the free will of humans. He never imposes His own. This was the case since the time of Adam and Eve, where He told him that they had all the trees and all the good things around them. He also told Adam that He was his Father, that he would care for him and that he was not to follow anyone else. However, Adam was free to do so.

"Now the serpent was more crafty than any of the wild animals the Lord God had made. He said to the woman, "Did God really say, 'You must not eat from any tree in the garden'?" The woman said to the serpent, "We may eat fruit from the trees in the garden, but God did say, 'You must not eat fruit from the tree that is in the middle of the garden, and you must not touch it, or you will die.'" Genesis 3:1

Poor Adam. The Serpent knew the weaknesses through which it could attack: beauty, seduction and creating doubt in the mind. The approach was wicked and cunning – and the question was rephrased. It was no longer about just a certain tree, but all the trees in the garden "You must not eat from any tree in the garden'?"

The major factor that influenced Adam was doubt and with his own free will, he followed the Serpent, and also with her own free will, Eve followed suit. As a result of their decision, both had to bear the consequences.

Our Lord said "how often I have longed to gather your children together, as a hen gathers her chicks under her wings, and you were not willing". He said this about Jerusalem after two thousand years sending them prophet after prophet and their preaching.

I am fearful that a day may come whereby the same is said to you that "you were not willing". When our Lord may say to you "Oh, my children how I yearned to you to call me 'our Father, who are in Heaven'. How I wanted to give you all the fruits of the Holy Spirit of Love, Joy, Peace and Patience. How I wanted to give you my whole love; I wanted to wash your sins; I wanted to give you my body and blood; I wanted to embrace you with all the divine fatherly tenderness. I wanted all this but you did not."

I want you to ask yourself this question: "Do you wish to be healed?" It is our chance to change the path of our whole life. It is a decision which needs courage and determination, leave the place in which you are now, disregard the frivolous material you may be reading, leave the place which is a stumbling block. I want to tell you something - throughout the New Testament, there was no one who followed Christ without giving up something. Matthew, do you wish to follow me? Then leave tax collection. Zaccaeus, do you wish to follow me? Then hurry up and come down from the tree. To the adulterous woman, do you wish to devote yourself to me? Then forsake your sinful past. He put a parting line in a person's life, delineating the old and the new.

Believe me the whole issue is quite simple. Christianity is not complicated. It is a simple matter of "Do you wish...?" Incidentally, the more you forsake, the greater is your love, because God whose love for us is great, knows to what extent is your love because:

"He who, being in the form of God, did not consider it robbery to be equal with God, but made Himself of no reputation, taking the form of a bondservant, and coming in the likeness of men. And being found in appearance as a man, He humbled Himself and became obedient to the point of death, even the death of the cross." Hebrews 2:8-15

This is a very great love that involves immense sacrifice.

We are spoilt, we wish to follow our Lord but without

any sacrifice, as the wealthy young who man pursued Christ was after eternal life. He was told to keep the commandments; which he said that he had kept them since childhood. Yet when it came to the sacrificing his wealth, it stopped there. Do you wish to reciprocate God's love? Then, sacrifice. One may say that they are willing to sacrifice, but I cannot part with this or that. It doesn't work that way. It is the letting go of that particular item of sentimental value that proves your love of God.

The book of Revelation 12:11 tells us about those who followed Jesus, "they did not love their lives so much as to shrink from death." And in the Praise Prayer we say "the Martyrs come bearing their tortures and the righteous come bearing their sufferings" meaning that each one of these come to the Lord with the offering of what they had given up.

O Lord, what have we given up for you? The sinful woman had given a great, great deal for Christ's sake, that is why He mentioned her saying: "Therefore I say to you, her sins, which are many, are forgiven, for she loved much. But to whom little is forgiven, the same loves little." (Luke 7:47)

As to a banquet you may give in honour of our Lord, it is not of significance. Simon the Pharisee did the same

and our Lord did not wish to turn down the invitation
lest he would embarrass Simon. Of course, Simon was
to be thanked as he spent a great deal on that banquet;
but as for the sinful woman, she gave up her profitable
livelihood.

Is it possible that today by you giving up something
to come to church, you feel that you are reaping the
blessing?

Do you wish to be healed? Seek The Lord. He heals, He
generously bestows the gifts of the Holy Spirit, He gives
you His own body and blood, He will renew you and will
create a new you.

"...go into your room, close the door and pray to your
Father, who is unseen. Then your Father, who sees
what is done in secret..." (Matt 6:6) He will bless you
with love for all people; just seek Him. He will bless
you with purity, sanctity and patience. Seek Him and
abandon earthly lures and He will give you the heavenly
kingdom. Do not tarry, He will give you everything. He
descended from the highest Heaven and all its glories
and was born in a humble manger for your sake.

We are used to seeking The Lord for petty issues.
Exams, children, ordeals you are suffering – but we
never consider "But seek first his kingdom and his

righteousness, and all these things will be given to you as well." (Matt 6:33)

Of course it is good that we seek our Lord in minor issues, but these should not be the main focus. The sinner woman gave up all her past and sought Him only, that is why He told her to go in peace and that her sins were forgiven, she felt reassured that she would never be abandoned.

I wish to draw your attention to a very important fact - those who had left behind everything and followed Jesus Christ, He took care of them to their last breath. As an example, Peter left behind his boat and followed Jesus and then became a fisher of men and the corner stone of the church.

Peter's nature also changed. One time Christ rebuked him "Away Satan", at another stage Peter denied Christ. He swore and cursed. It is said in history that during the last night prior to the crucifixion Peter ran away to avoid being crucified, perhaps likely to deny Christ for the second time. At the gates of Rome he came face to face with Christ "Where are you going Peter?" He told Jesus that he was scared. Jesus said "I will go to be crucified in your place for the second time.' Peter cried, turned back and when he was brought to the cross he requested to be crucified upside down, but upside down because he felt that he was unworthy to die the same way as Christ.

When Jesus Christ told Peter to "Follow me", Peter left everything and followed Christ and he became Christ's responsibility. When someone leaves everything and commits oneself to Christ, regardless of their human weaknesses, Christ takes over dealing with these weaknesses and He nurtures the soul, until we are safely home in Heaven.

Christ always asks if you wish to be healed. For example, someone like the Samaritan woman, what would her psychological state be? One would assume she would not be in a good state. But she was healed, because it was her wish.

To find peace within yourself, try to read the heavenly promises in the Gospel. This will give you reassurance, strength and blessings.

In regards to the paralytic man, this is a very sad situation to be in. There was no one to drop him in the pool when the Angel stirred it. Was it possible that there was no one compassionate enough to put him in there? Let us suppose you are in the same situation, you do not come from a loving family and you are there watching others being taken in by their family, and you there, thinking to yourself "there is no one to drop me in the pool"/ I tell you there are similar situations among us and within our churches. Would that be embarrassing? Yes, because compassion is on the decline.

Do you wish to be healed? The evangelistic movement within the church is stagnant. Why? I may say that perhaps some members of the congregation are not keen on their contact with Christ or perhaps they were not exposed to it.

Can you imagine the Samaritan woman when she ran evangelizing to everyone? Can you imagine the reaction of community? Possibly something similar to comments like: "Who are you to tell us? Did you forget who you are? Were you not the one who was married before and now you're not living with some one who is your husband? And now you come to preach us?" Perhaps she turned to say: "Please understand me, I am not here to talk about myself, nor am I here to preach to you. I am here to tell you about someone else, someone who told me everything about my past. Come, all I am asking you is to come and see for yourselves. I'm not forcing you. It is a treasure which I do not want you to miss on." And then after the lengthy and exhausting convincing they went with her. Then when the meeting took place, its impact was described in the Gospel.

This is what we call the evangelical movement within

the church. Those who submit their souls to The Lord and feel the freedom and joy of their contact with Him, become eager to share this joy with others. When Peter told Jesus "Go away from me, Lord; I am a sinful man!" Then Jesus said to Simon, "Don't be afraid; from now on you will be a fisher of men." (Luke 5:3-10) Of course Peter was taken by surprise, he did not realize that once he confessed his sins, the record of his sins was erased and the page became white and Christ who dwelled within him, designated him for His mission.

If we apply this to evangelism now, what is the approach to inviting people? Can you go to someone to ask if they want to join you and to establish a society or fellowship? Or say to them "Come and taste the richness of our Father's house? I'm not a notable person, just an average person, the same as you. But like the Samaritan Woman, I experienced the sweetness of the call. I want you to join me to taste the same sweetness... It is all in the Holy Book, come and taste the sweetness of the Bible. "

People will realize that you are sincere with no ulterior motives, and this was what our Preacher St. John said in his first epistle:

"That which was from the beginning, which we have heard, which we have seen with our eyes, by which we have looked at and our hands have touched—this we proclaim concerning the Word of life. The life appeared; we have seen it and testify to it, and we proclaim to you the eternal life, which was with the Father and has appeared to us. We proclaim to you what we have seen and heard, so that you also may have fellowship with us. And our fellowship is with the Father and with his Son, Jesus Christ. We write this to make our joy complete."

What did he mean by this? He wants us to taste the complete joy, which he tasted when he lived with Christ. I tell you, all those who tasted the life with Christ evangelized quietly and without fuss, because they acquired a new, pragmatic, quiet and Christian nature.

We have a real life example before us: The Samaritan Woman. Her reputation could not be described as being "beyond reproach". Some may have thought that she was not worth the effort, even her past would have been detrimental. I tell you her past was the most vital factor towards her evangelism. When her listeners witnessed the difference, what more incentive did they need? Perhaps, following their conversion, they also turned to evangelists.

When Zacchaeus, Head of Tax Collectors, gave half his wealth to the poor, people could not believe that drastic change in him. That man who made people suffer when he collected taxes from them, and had become so compassionate.

"I HAVE NO ONE TO DROP ME IN THE POOL"

On another note, when the paralytic was healed and he walked – putting aside the conversation between Christ and him and the nonsense of the Jews who blamed Christ for healing on the Sabbath. You and I share in the guilt of causing the hurt of the paralytic man in his plea "I have no one to drop me in the Pool". There are many people who are outside the Church and who have no one to drop them into the healing waters of the 'Church Pool'; that Pool of Grace. These people could be your neighbour, your colleague. You may start even through casual conversations, and they may open their hearts to you. Let me quote Christ "Don't you have a saying, 'It is still four months until harvest'? I tell you, open your eyes and look at the fields! They are ripe for harvest." (John 4:35)

Our Church has to move. I mean really move. It must have a motivating, inner energy, not a stagnant church that is content as it is, and all is sweet and fine, with services and activities which is mere talk. Who on the last day will stand before The Lord and say "Sir, I have no man to put me into the pool...." and they may add and "this is despite the fact that there was someone next to me who sat at a comfortable office, or there was someone who lived opposite, or even, there was someone who lived with me in the same house who knew You".

The Jews tried to incite the people claiming Christ broke the Law because He healed the paraplegic on the Sabbath "For this reason they tried all the more to kill him." Jesus gave them a calm reply "My Father is always at his work to this very day, and I too am working." (John 5:17) Meaning that the Heavenly Father is still working, even though it is the Sabbath. Christ revealed to us the mystery of the Father in relation to us. He works for us, constantly without cessation. And one may argue; why since He created the whole world, the angels are watchful, the forces of nature are in control, why is He constantly working?

"My Father is always at his work to this very day, and I too am working." This statement makes us reflect on a serious point regarding those who gave up everything to follow Christ and work under His name. Hence, they are bound to encounter tribulations on their way; similar to when the Pharisees rebuked Christ for "working on the Sabbath". Do not get involved in discussions, do not argue - block your ears and continue to carry out our Lord's work. How fruitful would it be if this were to be the nature of work within the Church instead of criticism? What is the main work of our Heavenly Father? Repentance through touching the heart or dropping the paraplegic in the Pool. Actions which bring joy both to you and to our Heavenly Father. The work grows and grows, and God's name is glorified. This is the soul's spiritual work.

When you bring souls and each soul clings to The Lord, you feel that God's work is growing. It is a continuous process. This must be our nature as God's children, we talk to him saying "Our father who are in Heaven..." since the time "the Spirit of God was hovering over the face of the waters." His Spirit dwelt within us, His Spirit is within the Church working daily through the sacraments, especially in the sacraments of Repentance and the Eucharist. We also work because our Heavenly Father is still working.

The Man Born Blind

The Last Sunday of the Great Lent

The last Sunday of the Great Lent is about the Man born blind, otherwise known as Baptism Sunday, which is appropriately named, because there is a link between human blindness and the spiritual blindness when a person is not in contact with Christ.

Christ says "I am the Light of the world" and so, to see the light, you need eyes of sound vision; but spiritual vision was obscured in the human being since the moment he sinned. He became unable to see God, while God was and is the same: He has not changed.

Perhaps one may say that the church constantly reminds us about sin, repentance, abstinence from committing evil, having a loving heart and living in peace. It is not only so, because we are not governed merely by a set of commandments and precepts, once observed we get our reward.

The actual fact is that we need to see God. We are able to see, but if one sees everything and is unable to see God, what is it worth? Adam's first and foremost joy was to hear the daily morning voice of God with the morning breeze. He saw God with his heart and through his inner being. He had cherished and rejoiced in that joy because not a day had passed without him hearing and seeing God, whom he saw through his heart, since God cannot be seen with human eyes but is seen through our hearts.

As I mentioned earlier the sequence of the Great Lent Sundays are not randomly set.

Now, following our reflection through these sequences, whatever takes place in our life we will be able to deal with it with open eyes. I am thinking of the man born blind and at the same time I am thinking of our situation after regaining the eyesight; probably the blind man was constantly worried that he might lose his eyesight again, and I have the same concern, what if we lose our regained eyesight? Let us assume that the blind man was possibly concerned that if his regained eyesight was just a glimpse of light.

Adam's blindness was self-inflicted, because he detached himself from God. He wanted to be separate from God; an independent entity. He was arrogant and proud for being able to know the difference between good and evil, similar to God. And so, had no need for our Lord's presence in his life.

The major human sin is the focusing on the ego, on one's status, and on one's pride. If we only reflect on Isaiah 2:22 - "Stop trusting in mere humans, who have but a breath in their nostrils. Why hold them in esteem?"

Self-Inflicted Blindness

As I said earlier, Adam blinded himself and lost his sight through his own fault. Jesus came with the purpose of re-opening his eyes. This was the same purpose regarding the one born blind. The previous Sunday spoke about the paraplegic man and he was told not to sin anymore, lest worse would happen to him. Jesus was asked, "Who was it that sinned? Was it he or his parents?" and Jesus answered that neither he nor his parents had sinned, it was for a divine purpose and that He was there to restore sight, which we commonly call enlightenment and for us the enlightenment is the through the sacrament of Baptism.

The one who is born from above is enlightened both in one's heart and one's life. Dust is not the only source of one's being, because spirituality cannot be seen through physical senses. Our Preacher Apostle Paul asks us to compare like with like, "This is what we speak, not in words taught us by human wisdom but in words taught by the Spirit, explaining spiritual realities with Spirit-taught words." (1 Corinthian 2:13) Meaning that if I wish to experience spirituality, I need to be spiritual.

The problem Christianity suffers from these days is that reaching Christ is not through intellectual persuasion, for example attempting to prove the oneness of the Trinity, or similar doctrines. Christianity's problem today, whether it be in the East or the West, is a materialistic problem. If the eyes are blind, how is it possible to see our Lord? God is the Light of the world. He came not only as the Light of the world, but also to open the closed eyes to enable people to see the Light, to reach Him and once that happens, people will know the meaning of happiness.

The ability of Christ to give us new life

I think we all agree that without Christ, life is dull, dark and worthless. If Christ is not present within us through every detail during our lifetime on this earth, then our life has no real value.

"Jesus answered and said to him, "Most assuredly, I say to you, unless one is born again, he cannot see the kingdom of God." Nicodemus said to Him, "How can a man be born when he is old? Can he enter a second time into his mother's womb and be born?" Jesus answered, "Most assuredly, I say to you, unless one is born of water and the Spirit, he cannot enter the kingdom of God. That which is born of the flesh is flesh, and that which is born of the Spirit is spirit. Do not marvel that I said to you, 'You must be born again.' The wind blows where it wishes, and you hear the sound of it, but cannot tell where it comes from and where it goes. So is everyone who is born of the Spirit." John 3:3-9

In the case of the born blind man, "He spat on the ground and made mud with saliva, then anointed the man's eyes and asked him to go and wash in the Pool of Siloam." (John 9:7)

When Jesus Christ asked him to go and wash in the Pool, He could have simply said "Open your eyes", yet

He asked him to go and wash in the Pool. Christ broke the rules of nature; He healed the man with a withered hand and told him "stretch out your hand". How could a man with a withered hand stretch his hand?

Sometime ago, I read a research carried out by a regrettably leading theologian. The research was about the subject of the man with the withered hand, whereby he stated that when the man stretched his hand it was because Jesus had in him the faculty of inducing self-intimation, which he exercised upon the man whereby the man stretched his hand. A withered hand to be stretched through the faculty of inducing self-intimation cannot be possible. It was through the power of Christ, the Creator. He used His power in both cases; the born blind whose eyes were created from mud, and the withered hand whose tissues were also miraculously created.

On another note, I want to ask you about an important point, why did He ask the born blind man to go and wash in the Pool? Meaning that vision would take place through the water. Believe me my dear friends, it is because we are already enjoying this Grace, we are taking it for granted. We are unable to appreciate the fact that a person whose eyes are not opened upon Jesus through Baptism is a lost person on earth. A person whose eyes are not open to see our Lord through reading the Gospel, leaves in darkness. You may say that we know that God exists, and we are aware that the Light exists. I know that you know, but the basic thing is the presence of the eyes which can see the Light.

God came to the world with His Message, as stated in Chapter one of the Gospel of our Preacher John, "In Him was life, and the life was the light of men. And the light shines in the darkness, and the darkness did not comprehend it." Therefore, the conflict was between "Darkness" and "Light". It was this same Light which shined in the eyes of the man born blind when his eyesight was restored.

The Pauline Epistle that is read on this day says, "Therefore put to death your members which are on the earth: fornication, uncleanness, passion, evil desire, and covetousness, which is idolatry. Because of these things the wrath of God is coming upon the sons of disobedience..." (Colossians 3:5)

Baptism is symbolic to our burial in Christ. For example, the Blind Man was expelled from his church the Jewish Synagogue. They reviled him and cast him out. He was insistent that his eyesight was restored and that he had seen Jesus. The Blind Man had actually gone through death-like periods. It was not easy.

Let us now imagine this situation occurring within our church, we expel someone from the church saying "Get out" or even go to the extent of calling the Caretaker to drag him out and if given a way, throw him in hell. This was the decision of the synagogue; this man had gone through death-like times. He must have roamed through the streets and when he saw Jesus, he leapt towards Him. "Jesus heard that they had cast him out; and when He had found him, He said to him, "Do you believe in the Son of God? He answered and said, "Who is He, Lord, that I may believe in Him?" And Jesus said to him, "You have both seen Him and it is He who is talking with you." Then he said, "Lord, I believe!" And he worshiped Him."

The man was eager to see more and more of Him.

The last verse in the ninth chapter of the Gospel of St John says: "I am the Good Shepherd". This means that Jesus had established an enclosure to keep his flock safely within. Those who are rejected by the world are safe among His flock. Those who are baptized are born again and join this flock as "Flesh gives birth to flesh, but the Spirit gives birth to spirit."

For this reason, fear should not have a place within our hearts. We are safe being among his pasture: "Do not be afraid, little flock, for your Father has been pleased to give you the kingdom." (Luke 12:32)

We need to be conscious of Christ's Grace. What is the reaction of the one who was unable to see, and is now able to see? Safeguard this gift by all means. Protect it against disease and anything that may expose the eyes to injury or may deprive from seeing Jesus. One would rather lose everything, rather than lose seeing Christ.

I warn you that once spiritual blindness enters into our hearts, we will lose Jesus. For example, if you tell me that you have a problem with your brother, that you'll never forgive him and it is it entirely his fault. For arguments sake, let us assume that all what you are saying is true, and you are harbouring this grudge in the depths of your heart, what is the outcome? The outcome is that you are losing the purity and peace within your heart. You are blind again and unable to see our Lord. For this reason, I am telling you my dearly beloved, you are custodians of the gift of the Light which our Lord entrusted you with. You need to protect this gift with all your might. We need to protect our spiritual wholeness the way it is handed to us by Christ.

Let us keep the whiteness of our baptismal garment as it was at our baptism. Let us keep it the way it was and if it gets stained, we wash it with Christ's blood which purifies us from all our sins. Today's Christians are required to be cautious because life is short and evil is rife, purity of the heart is hard to maintain. Please understand the fact that once darkness overshadows one's heart whether through earthly materialism, lust, grudges or extreme pressures or all of these - what is there left of our Christianity? What is our Baptism worth? What is the worth of all what was given to us? Just bear all these points in mind, and that now after your eyes are open, you are enjoying bountiful blessings. This is our Church, our property, I am our Lord's child and I confess this when I partake in His precious body and blood, because He died for my sake.

We gaze at the Cross and we say "You are mine. This God is my God". We all hold a great status which is conferred upon us. We need to safeguard our eyesight lest we lose seeing our Lord, after we were washed in the Pool of Siloam.

The other point which I hope will be a subject of our reflection was when "His disciples asked Him, saying, "Rabbi, who sinned, this man or his parents, that he was born blind?" Jesus answered, "Neither this man nor his parents sinned, but that the works of God should be revealed in him."

What is a portrait of compassion and humility that the works and Glory of God be made manifest through a lowly blind man

David the psalmist tell us of God's glory in the Creation, "The heavens declare the glory of God; the skies proclaim the work of his hands." So many times we spoke about God's glory in his creation - see the birds in the sky, the lilies in the fields, the mysteries researched by scientists, the functions of the human organs and the anatomy of the human body. His glory is manifested in countless ways.

We have discussed a new manner in which God's glory is manifested in our life. We thank you Jesus, that your glory may be manifested in us.

However, what is the impact of my theology in relation to the human being unless it is actually manifested in the human being. What is the point if I ascribe to our Lord a hundred names or even a thousand names? What does it mean to a person if I keep on describing how great He is in His creation and in the wonders of nature? We saw all this in the Old Testament, in the Psalms and in all the Praises.

Glorifying God in my own life

He had been glorified in all of those, but I want Him to be glorified in me, in my own weakness because I know

He can be glorified in me because He said so. He says that He is glorified in the weakest.

One time he had before him five thousand hungry men. He asked the disciples to feed them. The disciples, in frustration, asked how could they? They needed 100 dinars to feed this multitude. The whole situation was embarrassing. Somewhere, among the crowd there was an innocent little child with five loaves. Jesus asked this little child if he could have those 5 loaves and two fish for the multitude and the little child gave it to Him cheerfully. The child gave him everything he hand, withholding nothing. And so Jesus fed the multitude of five thousand men, and in addition the women and children because of the offering of this child.

In this case we can see God's glory did not require an important person, or someone wealthy or with status, nor did it need someone muscular and strong. God brought young David to face and eventually kill the Philistine giant, Goliath.

Today, the reassuring fact is that God is glorified within others: "Lord Jesus, this is the blessing I ask of you, that You be glorified in me and I glorify you because without you, I will be worth nothing more the handful of dust from which I was made. Be glorified in me O, Lord, as you were glorified in other saints before."

Jesus said that He is glorified in weakness. That does not mean that He is not also glorified in strength. I tell you something, He is glorified in a person even after death. As an example, we have St. Mina the Miraculous, who died and was thrown in the desert and after about three centuries of his death, there was a shepherd in the desert who used to walk his goats. Each time these goats had scabies, they rubbed themselves in the sand of that spot. They were healed. The king whose daughter suffered from a skin disease, heard about this. He sought help to see if this could alleviate his daughter's problem. At night the girl had a dream that St. Mina was buried in that spot.

This was St. Mina through whom God is glorified. A town was built in his name and around the whole world in Europe, Africa and Asia clay bottles containing water were found with the image of St. Mina drawn on them. This meant that his fame reached everywhere. What does that mean? When was God glorified in him? He was glorified in him after his death. This is the point I wish to emphasize.

How was God glorified in Abu Magar? It was said that he was falsely accused of sinning with a woman, who claimed that he was the culprit. He was dragged, was thrown flat on his face in the mud, was mocked "You pretend to be a priest, you pray and preach, then you commit such a serious sin. Now, you have to marry this girl and be her keeper." He obeyed and raised his grievance to The Lord. In a way, he considered it a blessing that he was going to be a recluse away from people, bearing in mind that these people were also happy because they caused him harm. They would not praise him anymore. It was a situation where a barrier was set between him and them, and a path opened between him and God.

When the time came for the girl to deliver the baby, it was divinely revealed to her that the infant would not be born and that she would remain in labour until she confessed the truth.

When his disciple ran to him told him that the whole village is on its way to vindicate you. He hurried to leave and said that the Lord had saved us from the first test, now Satan will make us fall into the trap of false praise. Again, the Lord is glorified even after death, because in this case the Blind Man reached the stage of death. It didn't have to be the actual physical death like St. Mina's case.

In His final words to His disciples, Jesus told them that

the Son of Man came to be glorified in the world. How would He be glorified? Through the love of the one who obeys Him. Our Lord's glory is within us, it is not boastful. After telling His Disciples this, he told them "Very truly I tell you, unless a kernel of wheat falls to the ground and dies, it remains only a single seed. But if it dies, it produces many seeds."

One may ask "Lord, How will I be glorified?" He would answer, "You must die, be buried and become a big tree, and I will do the same. I will die on the cross, thus my life begins".

For this reason, within the Church we believe that God's glory starts with stages of "mortification". We mortify our desires and each process of mortification is a glorification of our Lord. Is there a route that leads us to Jesus other than that of the cross? Is it possible to get rid of the cross and find another way? The Disciples tried, but he told them that that was the only way. Our God's glory could not be reached except through His crucifixion.

For this reason, my dearly beloved, each time we follow Christ's teachings when we avoid love of the world and when we mortify our lustful desires, a new love of God is born with us and we grow before His eyes, then we feel the actual glory. People will not notice, because this glory is not outwardly, but it is between God and us. When the Blind Man was born, no one gave him any status except Christ who told him that He was the one who had healed his eyes and for the blind man that was all he had wanted; that was his own glory.

Do you now believe that your only glory lies in Jesus? Will you mortify any other desire? If you lose everything and gain Christ, would you consider that a gain? "But what things were gain to me, these I have counted loss for Christ".

Be brave and say: "My share is The Lord. He is my glory." Christ said that He did not seek glory from people. On the contrary, people's glory is detrimental, it leads to pride and pride leads to egotism and Christ asks us to crucify the ego.

According to Christianity, our glory comes from crucifying the ego, it comes through the cross and death. This is what we call the glory of the Church.

When we talk about the glory of our church and the greatness of our forefathers, we say it was a poor church - it was a church of martyrs, persecuted throughout the world, it was a self-denying and ascetic church. There were those who loved Christ the King so much that they lived in mountains and caves, and we keep repeating this, but this glory had one path; that of the cross.

Furthermore, next to mortification and the carrying of the cross, there are no two ways to glory, only one way and that is for our Lord Jesus to touch our eyes and anoint them as He did with the Blind Man. And unless Jesus touches us, we cannot feel the glory. Do you know when they say about someone that 'dust turns into gold in his hand'? What will I be transformed into when I am placed in Christ's hand? What will become of me if I receive one of Jesus' sweet touches; touching my heart, my thoughts and my life?

O Lord Jesus, I need to touch you even if I touch the border of your garment, similar to the woman who suffered from the flow of blood, similar to the sinful woman whose eyes were flowing with tears and you made her heart flow with love. I yearn for your touch.

My dearly beloved, how much time have we wasted throughout our lives, whereby we could have made contact with our Lord's word, His Gospel and His teachings? Instead we preferred to be in touch with everything else except Christ's word. Our glory is in attaching ourselves to our Lord. If we attach ourselves to a worthless person, that is what we tend to become, and by the same token if we attach ourselves to a great person, that's what we tend to become. What about when one becomes attached to our infinite Lord? That is why Prophet David says "But as for me, it is good to be near God".

Being near God or being attached to God, is a very profound theological expression, because since we are living in a time of Grace, we are now members of the body of Christ.

The expression itself is not a metaphor; it is actual. For this reason when Christ speaks of the Sacrament of Matrimony within the Church, outsiders are unable to understand this concept. Thus, they marry two, three, or four. Ours is a sacramental mystery. In his epistle to the Ephesians, Apostle Paul says "Husbands, love your wives, as Christ loved the church and gave himself up for her, that he might sanctify her". This mystery is profound, and I am saying that it refers to Christ and the church because we are members of His body.

In another instance Christ says that He is the head. Apostle Paul also says about Christ that he is the Head and that we are His body. We all know what is the head in relation to the body and there is no need to elaborate on its function. If the head is separated from the body, what is the body worth? Nothing. Similarly, without Christ we end to be the same.

Therefore, my dearly beloved, Christ's touch of the man born blind created new opened eyes whereby the man, who was given new sight, became attached to The Lord.

May The Lord give us the same blessing that each moment and each minute, we stand before Him in prayer from the depth of our heart, or when we read the Gospel, may this be a time of attachment to The Lord and spiritual growth.

Each time we silently stand before the cross, we are attached to Christ and His glories. Our lifetime on this earth is short regardless of how long it is. We need time with our Lord so that we may grow. For this reason the old Egyptian Iconographer whenever he drew the image of a saint he would drew the image with a large halo, but Christ's image was drawn with a cross at its background and that is how we differentiate between the two. However, when he drew Judas' image, he did so without the halo. Also, each time the Coptic Iconographer drew the image of a saint, he depicted the saint 'larger than life'. For example, St. George's image is quite large, but his horse was small in comparison. This was to demonstrate that the person grew in grace when they were attached to God, even if ostracized by the world.

The first priority is to have God glorified in our own life, which is quite possible knowing that the way to glory is through mortification and walking in the path of the cross. The kernel of the wheat harvests a vast crop once it is buried in the soil. The path to glory is through Jesus' touch, which is a great honour.

What a blessing when our Lord is glorified in my home and in my household

What a blessing when the whole Household is attached to our Lord. As soon as you step into the house you sense the fragrance of love, self-denial and endurance. You sense the fragrance of Christ's presence. You can see that their countenances bear Christ's image, and you can't help thinking "Christ is glorified among this household". What more can anyone ask for?

Again, God is glorified in weakness. There are so many whose vision is 'twenty/twenty', but Christ chose to be glorified in this weak man because that was also what Christ had told Paul "My grace is sufficient for you, for my power is made perfect in weakness."

St Paul became a malleable tool in our Lord's hand. He was tested and God was glorified in his weakness, illness and weariness more than his previous strength before he came to know Christ. What do you think about the fact that the first time God was glorified in him was when God had blinded him? When Paul was en route what happened to him when Christ appeared to him while he was on his way? He was blinded; He was blinded of his whole past. St Paul asked what was he supposed to do and the Lord told him how He would be glorified in him. The Disciples complained but Jesus said, "I will show him how much he must suffer for my name" and how he would place him before many Governors and Kings who will make him suffer. The fragrance of Christ was to be manifested in him.

When St Paul was blinded he felt lost, he didn't know where to go or what to do and Jesus directed him to Ananias. He told him to go to the Church take his guidance from there. So he went to Ananias, he believed and was baptized and only then the scales fell off his eyes, similar to being washed in the Pool of Siloam.

Paul was a man of status and education, both within his synagogue and within his position. God could have been glorified in Paul's authority and status. But, no. God chose to be glorified in his weakness, when he was dragged from house to house, feeling his way until his eyes were opened upon Christ.

In brief, my dearly beloved, we pray that God is glorified in our lives. He came as the Light of the world and an eye opener. He blessed us with his wisdom, so let us nurture it. Let us walk, each one of us, through our path of the cross. Carrying our cross lovingly and joyously, observing our mortification of the flesh against all the worldly lures, always seeking Jesus' touch in our lives. Let us say with Prophet David "I will bless the Lord who guides me; even at night my heart instructs me. I know the Lord is always with me. I will not be shaken, for He is right beside me."

We will go even beyond David, we will pray "Lord, we are members of your body, please do not let this member be detached from you. You are the vine and we are the branches. We are the flesh of your flesh. We are the bones of your bones. What greater glory are we to seek?"

May our Good Lord and Saviour Jesus Christ be glorified within each of us, so that we may open our hearts to Him. May he help us retain the spiritual blessings we received in our Baptism.

GLORY BE TO OUR GOD FOREVER AND EVER. AMEN.

CPSIA information can be obtained
at www.ICGtesting.com
Printed in the USA
LVHW031451270223
740495LV00004B/266